PSYCHIC EMPOW
"…a must re

ABOUT THE AUTHOR

Joe H. Slate is a licensed psychologist and founder of the International Parapsychology Research Foundation. He is Professor Emeritus at Athens State College, Alabama, where he served as Head of the Division of Behavioral Sciences, and Director of Institutional Effectiveness. He is Honorary Professor at Montevallo University and Adjunct Professor at Forest Institute of Professional Psychology. After completing his Ph.D. at the University of Alabama, Dr. Slate punctuated his training with additional study in hypnosis and somatoform disorders at the University of California. His research interests, while focusing on psychic empowerment, have involved him in a wide range of health-related studies, including stress management, wellness, pain management, and rejuvenation. Dr. Slate's research has been funded by the U. S. Army Missile Research and Development Command, Huntsville, Alabama; the Parapsychology Foundation, New York City; and numerous private sources.

TO WRITE TO THE AUTHOR

If you wish to contact the author or would like more information about this book, please write to the author in care of Llewellyn Worldwide, and we will forward your request. Both the author and publisher appreciate hearing from you and learning of your enjoyment of this book and how it has helped you. Llewellyn Worldwide cannot guarantee that every letter written to the author can be answered, but all will be forwarded. Please write to:

Llewellyn's New Worlds of Mind and Spirit
P.O. Box 64383, Dept. K635-1, St. Paul, MN 55164-0383, U.S.A.
Please enclose a self-addressed, stamped envelope for reply, or $1.00 to cover costs. If outside U.S.A., enclose international postal reply coupon.

Strategies for Success

PSYCHIC EMPOWERMENT

A 7-DAY PLAN FOR SELF-DEVELOPMENT

JOE H. SLATE, PH.D.

1997
Llewellyn Publications
St. Paul, Minnesota 55164-0383, U.S.A.

FIRST EDITION
Third Printing, 1997

Cover Design: Tom Grewe
Cover Image © 1995 Photo Disc, Inc.
Photography: Michael Ray Norris
Book Design and Layout: Designed To Sell

Library of Congress Cataloging-in-Publication Data
Slate, Joe H.
    Psychic empowerment: a 7-day plan for self-development / Joe H. Slate.
       p.   cm. — (Strategies for success)
    Includes bibliographical references and index.
    ISBN 1-56718-635-1 (paperback : alk. paper)
    1. Success—Psychic aspects.   I. Title.   II. Series.
  BF1045.S83S5 1995
    131—dc20
                                      95-1543
                                        CIP

Publisher's note:
Llewellyn Worldwide does not participate in, endorse, or have any authority or responsibility concerning private business transactions between our authors and the public.

    All mail addressed to the author is forwarded but the publisher cannot, unless specifically instructed by the author, give out an address or phone number.

Llewellyn Publications
A Division of Llewellyn Worldwide, Ltd.
P.O. Box 64383
St. Paul, Minnesota 55164-0383, U.S.A.

About Llewellyn's "Strategies for Success" Series

The secret to success is really no secret at all. Just ask any successful person. The "secret" is really a universal truth that belongs to each and every human being on the planet. That truth is: Success begins in the Mind.

Many of us live from day to day feeling that "something" is missing, or that we are a victim of circumstances that make success impossible.

The greatest barrier to success is this illusion of helplessness and powerlessness. It is the illusion that you have no choices in life. The successful person knows that this illusion is like a deadly virus to the spirit.

The good news is that you possess the power—inside yourself now—to sweep illusions from your mind and begin using your mind for what it was intended: to lift human consciousness to a higher plane and make this planet a better place for yourself and your children.

How is this done?

That's where Llewellyn's "Strategies for Success" come in. Techniques are available that can help you activate your inner resources to create exciting new potentials in your life. Some of these techniques involve the promotion of psychic empowerment.

Psychic empowerment concepts and strategies recognize that the source of ultimate power resides within the Mind. Whether a simple affirmation or a complex empowering procedure, each strategy embodies a firm regard for the divine spark of greatness existing in everyone.

Your psychic faculties are standing behind the door of consciousness. With the techniques presented in this book, you can open the door and enjoy a success beyond your wildest dreams.

Success is your destiny. When you are self-empowered, you become the sole architect of your life. Why wait? Seize your power now.

TABLE OF CONTENTS

LIST OF ILLUSTRATIONS

LIST OF CHARTS

ACKNOWLEDGMENTS

To the many people who have contributed to the production of this book, I wish to express my heartfelt thanks. I am especially grateful to my students whose seminal thinking helped shape this project and sharpen my own conclusions. Many of their valuable suggestions have found their way into this volume.

With a deep sense of gratitude and admiration, I would like to thank my learned colleagues who were collaborators, reviewers, and critics for many sections of this book.

To the International Parapsychology Research Foundation, for nurturing this project and actively promoting research and the discovery of new knowledge, I will always be grateful.

PREFACE

This book is about the power of the mind. It probes the mind's psychic faculties and the human capacity to access higher planes of psychic power. It goes beyond the mere presentation of information and beliefs about psychic phenomena, to offer rational explanations of the "unexplained," and to focus on the personal benefits of the psychic experience. Through the systematic development of the Psychic Empowerment Perspective, the book reveals the empowering nature of a wide range of psychic phenomena—from simple telepathy to out-of-body experiences, and from automatic writing to table tilting—while at the same time formulating a host of innovative, psychic empowerment procedures.

The psychic empowerment perspective presented here recognizes that the incomparable worth of all human beings and faith in the human potential for greatness are essential conditions for becoming individually and globally empowered.

The strategies outlined in this book include a variety of techniques and procedures designed to stimulate our inner psychic growth and activate our highest psychic powers. In its probe of the higher planes of psychic power, the book strikes a balance between objective observation and practical application. Although its constant thrust is toward personal empowerment, the book takes into account an emergent globalization process and the empowering potential of psychic concepts on a global scale.

Part Three of the book presents the 7-Day Psychic Empowerment Plan, which organizes the seminal concepts of psychic empowerment into an accelerated, step-by-step program for psychic growth and development.

The ultimate end of psychic empowerment is twofold: First, to increase our insight and promote our own development; and second, to make the world a better place for present and future generations. Meeting that challenge is a major goal of this book.

INTRODUCTION
THE NATURE OF PSYCHIC EMPOWERMENT

Psychic empowerment is a continuous process of growth and self-discovery. When we are psychically empowered, we become increasingly aware of the boundless power within ourselves and the unlimited possibilities and opportunities around us. Through psychic empowerment, we unleash vast inner sources of new growth potential and achieve new levels of personal fulfillment. We lift consciousness to a higher plane and make this planet a better place for ourselves and our children.

The concept of psychic empowerment is based on this three-fold premise:

1. Within each of us is an abundance of untapped power and underdeveloped potential.

2. We can access and activate these inner resources to empower our lives.

3. Through that empowering process, we can literally create exciting, new potentials in our lives. The result is an upward spiral of personal growth which empowers and enriches us.

Almost everyone recalls some form of empowering psychic experience. Common examples are dreams that came true, intuitions that proved accurate, or simple experiences of *déjà vu*. Psychic experiences are so common among so many people, that we no longer consider them paranormal or extraordinary. Yet, questions concerning the nature of psychic phenomena persist, primarily because psychic experiences seem to lie outside our conventional explanations of human behavior. Furthermore, psychic phenomena are typically spontaneous, and do not readily lend themselves to objective analysis and empirical study: Precognitive dreams are reported by about three-fourths of all college students, but research efforts to generate and verify them in the laboratory have not been fully successful. Similarly, telepathic communication occurs so frequently that many of us consider it a normal part of our daily interactions, but laboratory efforts to demonstrate telepathy, even among individuals who report it as a common occurrence, have not consistently validated the phenomenon. Nevertheless, the documented instances of precognition, telepathy, and other forms of psychic phenomena, both in the laboratory and in everyday life, are so numerous that, when viewed objectively, they leave little room for doubt that these events do indeed occur.

The evolving body of evidence for psychic phenomena demands a careful re-examination of our thinking and a restructuring of our traditional views about human life and experience. The fact that the mind seems capable of experiencing realities beyond the known limits of sensory perception challenges our conventional systems and raises new questions about the nature of reality and human existence itself.

Critical to our personal development and better understanding of ourselves is an open, but vigilant mind that can objectively assess and accommodate new knowledge, even though it may contradict our old ways of thinking. Our personal empowerment requires exposure to diverse opinions and contradictory ideas. The result is a constant flow of new knowledge that, when seriously considered and integrated into the self system, becomes liberating and empowering, but when arbitrarily rejected, becomes constricting and disempowering. Therefore, a recognition of knowledge from many sources is essential in our struggle for self-understanding and full self-empowerment.

THE PSYCHIC EMPOWERMENT PERSPECTIVE

Among the most critical sources of empowering new knowledge is the psychic experience. The traditional focus on the mysterious side of psychic phenomena is finally giving way to an emergent emphasis on logical explanations and practical strategies to access valuable knowledge and promote the quality of human life, while at the same time contributing to global needs. We experience our world through sensory mechanisms and sensory-based perceptions that are cognitively organized, a process that is dependent on biological mechanisms. Psychic experience, on the other hand, reaches beyond known sensory and cognitive functions, thus augmenting sensory experience, while suggesting totally new alternatives for expanding awareness and acquiring knowledge. Examples of these are telepathy, precognition and retrocognition, clairvoyance, out-of-body experiences, and discarnate survival phenomena. Taken together, these phenomena suggest four major empowering principles:

1. The essence of our existence transcends biological or physical experience alone.

2. With the conventionally prescribed limits of human experience removed, the potentials for human growth and knowledge are significantly expanded.

3. We can dramatically increase our scope and store of knowledge by developing our psychic capacities.

4. Psychic self-empowerment and self-fulfillment are reasonable expectations for everyone.

A major challenge facing us today is a riveting, demystifying probe of the so-called paranormal that will explain its nature and unleash its empowering potentials. The psychic experience, whether voluntary or involuntary, is always empowerment driven. Discovering its capacity for empowerment requires attention to the psychic event and understanding of its significance. For example, many of our dreams are psychic and potentially empowering, but benefiting from the dream requires first recalling the dream, then understanding its message, and in some instances, acting upon it. The problem-solving dream challenges us by providing, in disguise, the raw material we need for a solution. Discovering the solution requires imagination and diligence in unraveling the dream, interpreting its symbols, and creatively applying its message.

The empowering effects of the psychic experience can be profound and enduring. They often involve the critical issues of our existence and our ultimate destiny. To disregard such phenomena, or to shrug them off as inconsequential, is to negate their empowering capacity to promote our growth and expand our range of knowledge and experience.

THE PSYCHIC EMPOWERMENT HIERARCHY

When we are psychically empowered, our multiple faculties function in a dynamic hierarchy that is constantly evolving and rearranging itself. Those abilities required for immediate coping spontaneously rise within the hierarchy to assume an appropriate place of prominence, thereby meeting our empowerment needs of the moment. Those abilities not in immediate demand descend in the hierarchy, but remain in reserve for future use as needed. In other words, our inner faculties are placed "on line" within a psychic system that is responsive to our empowerment needs, even those we do not consciously anticipate. This precognitive feature of the hierarchical system is a major characteristic of the psychically empowered individual. When initiative is required, the hierarchical system activates it. When courage is needed, the empowerment hierarchy delivers it. When creativity is demanded, the hierarchy reorganizes to generate it. When such practical skills as problem solving or analytical evaluation are called for, the empowerment hierarchy shifts its order to effectively access them. In situations involving danger, the empowerment hierarchy creates a shield of protection, and delivers the power needed to cope effectively with threatening situations. The resources required for wellness, stress management, habit control, and personal enrichment exist within a hierarchy that is responsive to the empowered self's multiple, changing demands.

Although our empowerment hierarchy functions spontaneously, at times it requires deliberate activation to meet certain situational demands or personal growth needs. When psychically empowered, we can access the hierarchical system and call forth specific inner resources at will. Achieving that empowered state demands mastery of many psychic empowerment strategies.

PSYCHIC EMPOWERMENT STRATEGIES

A major focus of this book is on workable strategies designed to unleash our psychic powers. As a growth process, psychic empowerment requires the exploration and practice of many approaches to discover those that work best for us individually. Some of the strategies presented in this book are designed to promote a general state of psychic readiness, whereas others are structured to activate specific psychic faculties. Each strategy is unique and can be practiced independently of other strategies; however, they share three common features: self-discovery, commitment, and investment.

Self-discovery

Psychic self-empowerment is possible only when we discover our inner psychic potentials and responsibly liberate them to work for ourselves and others. In undiscovered form, our psychic faculties seek expression and recognition through numerous indirect channels. They stand at the door of consciousness and knock, but they do not intrude—they make no forced entries. Sadly, to reject these psychic overtures is to close the door to self-discovery and a vast wealth of empowering possibilities.

Commitment

Through commitment to develop our psychic side, we liberate ourselves to achieve the highest levels of self-enlightenment and fulfillment. With unlimited psychic resources at our command, we can shape our own destiny while contributing to the common good. Only through psychic channels can we meet some of the world's most pressing needs. World peace, for example, must eventually flow not from the destructive wizardry of futuristic war technology, but from the positive power of raised global consciousness, and a firm commitment to global harmony.

Investment

Developing our psychic resources demands personal investment in the pursuit of new knowledge and psychic fulfillment. Although some psychic activity will occur effortlessly or spontaneously, the full actualization of our psychic potential requires diligence in developing empowering skills. Even the psychically gifted find that hard work is essential in fine-tuning their skills. Fortunately, a very modest investment in the psychic realm will often yield a generous payoff: The inner, knowing part of the self appears constantly poised to reward even a nominal probe of its empowering capacity.

The strategies of psychic empowerment developed in this book are anchored in a clear recognition of the dignity and incomparable worth of all human beings. Whether a simple affirmation of power, or a complex empowering procedure, each strategy embodies a firm regard for the divine spark of greatness existing in everyone. Among the most empowering strategies known are affirmations such as:

> *I am a person of worth; Success is my destiny;*
> *I am empowered.*

These affirmations are made even more powerful when they are accompanied by faith in ourselves, hope for the future, and love for others. Together, faith, hope, and love form the foundation upon which we can build an empowered life that simply cannot fail.

From the global perspective, psychic empowerment suggests new strategies for promoting a higher plane of global actualization. Global issues of poverty, homelessness, crime, hunger, human and animal suffering, and war are vital concerns of the psychically empowered. These problems require a firm commitment of our resources and energies toward making the world a better place. The abuse of human and animal rights, inequality in educational and economic opportunities, environmental pollution, loss of species, and reckless exploitation of the earth's resources demand our involvement, because our globe and the survival of future generations are now at risk.

Our self-empowerment rests largely on our willingness to accommodate the psychic experience and integrate it into our lives. By personally experiencing the psychic event, we come to know our psychic side and the empowering potential of psychic phenomena. The psychic experience is an important and convincing teacher, because it validates our psychic nature and connects us to the inner, knowing part of the self. It can advance us to a new level of self-understanding and appreciation of life as an exciting, endless journey of growth and discovery.

The psychic empowerment concepts and strategies presented in this book recognize the sources of ultimate power as residing within the self. Delegated power, whatever its origin, becomes real power only when internalized, integrated, and finally validated by the self. Likewise, such concepts as Universal Power, Cosmic Oneness, and Divine Power become personally empowering only when experienced as realities by the responsive, choosing self. In becoming self-empowered, there can be no substitute for personal autonomy and choice. Within each of us is the capacity to change the present and shape the future. When we are self-empowered, we are the sole architects of our destiny.

PART ONE

Extrasensory Perception

AN OVERVIEW

❧ I ❧

Extrasensory perception (ESP) is one of our most valuable channels for experiencing the inner and outer realities of our existence. The ESP potential exists in everyone, but it often lies dormant or repressed. ESP is important to our self-empowerment because it increases our capacity for awareness and expands our world of knowledge. Through ESP, we can explore, contact, and interact with important new sources of empowerment which otherwise would remain unavailable to us.

ESP is the knowledge of, or response to, events, conditions, and situations independently of our known sensory mechanisms or processes. It provides a channel that can by-pass normal sensory functions to directly engage realities and to experience them regardless of sensory stimulation. Sensory experience is limited by the capacity of our sensory mechanisms to respond to physical stimulation. Perception is usually seen as our interpretation of that physical stimulation. The intensity of the stimulation and our individual thresholds for responding to it become critical determinants in our biological capacity to experience reality. ESP, on the other hand, transcends the limitations of sensory experience and perception, and enables us to experience realities—past, present, and future—in a psychic mode that is not limited by the intensity or even the presence of sensory stimulation or any other known physiological parameter.

Rather than a poor substitute for sensory perception, ESP is often just as enriched and detailed. For example, psychic awareness of a future event can emerge as a factual, complete representation consisting of thought alone, or it can involve meaningful, realistic mental images that are intricate, colorful, and complete. Similarly, clairvoyant impressions are frequently accompanied by clear, mental pictures of distant realities unfolding in the psychic mind. Likewise, telepathic communications can include mental images that complement the purely cognitive content of the psychic sending and receiving process.

In contrast to ESP, psychokinesis (PK) operates to influence matter rather than to access information, but it may also employ certain ESP faculties. Examples of PK in our daily lives include our ability to mentally shape events or to influence the outcomes of situations, as well as our unexplained capacity to exercise superhuman powers in emergencies. In its broadest and perhaps most advanced form, PK encompasses our capacity to influence the biological body by channeling our mental powers to repair damaged tissue, restore normal organ functions, and promote health and wellness. In that capacity, PK often involves visualization of the physical body as well as clairvoyance, which can provide useful information about bodily functions. These are highly complex areas of psychic phenomena, but because their empowerment potentials are so great, we must consider them relevant and essential in our quest for psychic empowerment.

It is important to note that ESP can function at both conscious and subconscious levels of awareness. At the conscious level, we can experience awareness that is direct and free of distortions. However, the subconscious mind often is the mediator for psychic input, and messages received in the subconscious can be conveyed to conscious awareness either directly as clear psychic impressions, or indirectly through psychic dreams and revealing slips of the tongue or pen.

Psychic messages rising from the subconscious are often disguised through symbolism or distortion, challenging us to explore their significance and unravel their hidden meanings. Unfortunately, many messages of psychic significance remain within the subconscious, and many sources of psychic empowerment lie dormant there as well; because of either our reluctance to explore that part of ourselves or our inattentiveness to the often subtle empowering efforts of our subconscious mind. Many of the techniques presented in this book are formulated specifically to tap into the subconscious and maximize its empowering capacity.

Estimates of the extent of development of our inner potential are around 10 percent. The remaining 90 percent is largely psychic in nature, as attested to by the frequent and varied manifestations of spontaneous ESP in our daily lives. Premonitions, psychic intuitions, and precognitive dreams are reflections of psychic power within the subconscious mind. That power in its suppressed, dormant form is like a butterfly in a bottle. Trapped and immobilized, the butterfly offers only a limited glimpse of its exquisite beauty and power. With its wings creased and its actions constricted, it seeks release and struggles for freedom. When finally liberated, it unfolds its wings with unparalleled grace and ascends in magnificent splendor. Like the majestic butterfly, our psychic potentials, once liberated, are emboldened to soar in a brilliant unfolding of infinite power and beauty.

ESP consists of three major abilities: telepathy, clairvoyance, and precognition. Telepathy, often called mind-to-mind communication, is the psychic sending and receiving of mental elements that can include both thought and emotional content. Clairvoyance, on the other hand, functions independently of another mind, and consists of the psychic perception of objects, conditions, situations, or current happenings. Precognition, the third type of ESP, is the extrasensory awareness of future events.

The following concepts typically characterize ESP experiences:

- Goal-orientation. When the goal of the ESP experience is identified, its potential for empowerment is magnified significantly.

- The absence of sensory stimulation. A state of reduced arousal, such as relaxation and mental passivity, will typically facilitate the ESP event.

- Imagery skills. Considered essential to a wide range of psychic functions, mental imagery practice will often accelerate development of ESP faculties.

- An interaction of conscious and subconscious elements, which promote our psychic growth and facilitate ESP.

- Either spontaneous or voluntarily induction of ESP. In its voluntary form, it is deliberately accessed and activated, usually through acquired psychic strategies.

ESP STRATEGIES

ESP strategies are designed to access and activate ESP faculties while promoting development of full psychic potential. Whether to activate inner potential to generate psychic power, or simply to tap into existing sources of psychic knowledge, practice is essential, because it builds the general conditions for psychic success while strengthening specific psychic skills. Among the most effective practice strategies are: empowering self-talk designed to generate an empowered mental state; cognitive relaxation to induce a responsive biological state; and mental imagery to heighten psychic readiness and sharpen specific psychic faculties. These strategies, as detailed in the following discussion, can promote psychic growth while establishing the foundation for a rich and more fully empowered life.

Psychic Empowerment Self-talk

Positive self-talk is a powerful strategy for generating an empowered mental state and building psychic competence. Because self-talk initiates a self-contained, self-empowered, sending and receiving communication system, it can be viewed as an inner form of empowering telepathy. Unlike conventional telepathy, self-talk is mind-to-mind communication in which the formulating, sending, and receiving process is managed exclusively by the self. In common usage, the term "telepathy" denotes mind-to-mind communication between two people, the sender and the receiver. Because it is self-contained, self-talk as inner-telepathy has empowering possibilities that greatly exceed conventional telepathy. Through inner-telepathy, latent, subconscious potentials can be awakened, and a host of subconscious mechanisms can be activated. The result is a dramatic increase in awareness and personal power. It is important to emphasize, however, that if unattended, self-talk can have disempowering consequences. Negative self-messages can block psychic functions, dilute inner power resources, and inhibit personal growth. A positive self-message will consistently overpower any of its negative opposites, so empowering self-talk demands diligence in forming strong self-messages, which intercept and neutralize disempowering communications.

Becoming psychically empowered requires positive self-talk which is both general and specific. General self-talk targets general goals or collective inner psychic functions. Specific self-talk focuses on either a precise goal or a particular psychic faculty. General self-talk is critical to psychic empowerment, because it initiates a comprehensive state of empowerment readiness and a success orientation conducive to more specific empowering self-talk.

The following passages illustrate both general and specific empowering self-talk. They can be used as effective practice and conditioning affirmations for building a continuous state of general empowerment and activating specific psychic faculties.

GENERALIZED EMPOWERMENT SELF-TALK

Day by day, I am becoming more fully aware of my psychic potentials. I am discovering ways of developing them to their peaks. My inner psychic faculties are constantly interacting and balancing each other. They are now at my command, under my direction, generating the power I need to influence events and achieve goals. I am now empowered to initiate inner functions and specific capacities at will. I am constantly empowered to be all that I need to be both physically and mentally.

SPECIFIC EMPOWERMENT SELF-TALK—PRECOGNITION

The future is now at my command. I can probe it to gain knowledge and increase awareness. My precognitive powers are like giant antennae that tap into the future. All the information I need is available to me. Precognitive knowledge will enable me to plan more effectively, make more responsible choices, and when necessary, avert future misfortune. Armed with precognitive insight, I am empowered to alter the present and shape the future. Precognitive wisdom empowers me to face the future with confidence and to effectively engage its boundless opportunities.

Specific Empowerment Self-talk—Telepathy

My life is now enriched because I am constantly empowered to interact and communicate mentally, both within myself and with others. Through telepathy, I have immediate access to the most advanced communication system known. I can use that system at will to expand awareness of myself and others. My powers to send and receive telepathically are constantly at my command.

Specific Empowerment Self-talk—Clairvoyance

Through clairvoyance, my awareness of myself and the universe is expanded. Clairvoyance enriches my life with new knowledge and unlimited thresholds for new experiences. Through clairvoyance, I can transcend at will the limitations of sensation and space to experience distant, unseen realities. With the boundaries of my existence dissolved, the possibilities for increased awareness are unlimited. Clairvoyance is the information vehicle that connects me to all I need to know. I am now receptive to clairvoyant knowledge, and I will use it wisely.

Positive self-talk can be effectively applied to access a host of other specific psychic faculties, including out-of-body travel and psychokinesis (PK).

Cognitive Relaxation

The second essential strategy for building psychic skills is cognitive relaxation, which is based on the capacity of the mind to relax the body. Relaxation skills enable us to assume command of not only our psychic faculties, but a host of biological functions as well. As a mind-over-body technique, cognitive relaxation can promote an empowered state of both physical and mental well-being.

The most effective relaxation procedure combines muscle relaxation, related mental imagery, and positive affirmations. The Finger Spread Procedure was devised to organize these elements into a strategy for releasing tension and promoting a mental state conducive to psychic empowerment. The Toe Lift Technique is designed to induce a deep state of physical relaxation; and finally, the Finger Interlocking Technique aids in stress management.

THE FINGER SPREAD PROCEDURE

Step 1   Spread the fingers of both hands and hold them in the tense spread position. Note the tension in the hands radiating into the arm muscles. Continue holding the finger spread position as the muscles become increasingly tired, then slowly relax the fingers. Take plenty of time for the relaxation to spread gradually over the hands and into the muscles of the arms and shoulders. With eyes closed, permit the relaxation to flow into your chest and central trunk region, then throughout your entire body.

Step 2 Create a mental image of a favorite, tranquil scene, as you permit relaxation to go deeper and deeper into the muscles and joints of your body.

Step 3 Conclude the exercise with the affirmation:

> I am fully relaxed and in command of all my inner powers.

Follow this with any specific affirmation you wish to give yourself regarding a particular goal.

TOE LIFT TECHNIQUE

Step 1 Lift the toes of both feet and hold them in the lift position as you slow your breathing. If you are wearing shoes, press your toes gently against the tops of the insides of the shoes.

Step 2 Tense the muscles in your feet and legs as you continue to hold the toe-lift position for a few moments, while breathing slowly and deeply.

Step 3 Slowly relax your toes, feet, and legs, as you give yourself the simple suggestion:

> I now give myself permission to become more and more fully relaxed.

Step three of this procedure can be expanded to include additional self-affirmations:

> My psychic powers are becoming stronger and stronger. I am now empowered to achieve my goal of (specify goal).

Finger Interlocking Technique

Finger Interlocking Technique

Step 1   Take a few deep breaths, exhaling slowly.

Step 2   Join the thumb and middle finger of each hand.

Step 3   Bring the hands together to form interlocking circles with the thumbs and middle fingers. Relax both hands as you give yourself the affirmation:

*I am now completely relaxed. I am in a state of
complete balance. I am tranquil, confident,
and secure.*

This technique can be practiced almost anywhere, for instance, before or during a speech, interview, test, or other potentially stressful situation. It can be implemented in seconds, with tremendously empowering results.

The Finger Interlocking Technique is important to our psychic empowerment because it not only generates a relaxed state, it can also protect the psychic system from depletion by creating a temporarily closed energy system. As thoughts are turned inward in that closed psychic state, new psychic energies can be generated through empowering affirmations such as:

*I am now energized with abundant psychic
power. My psychic potentials are free to unfold.
My psychic faculties are now activated.*

This brief procedure, employed prior to the application of psychic powers, tends to heighten psychic effectiveness and ensure better control of psychic faculties.

Another highly useful relaxation and ESP-conditioning exercise is the Peripheral Glow Procedure, which not only induces a relaxed state, but also sharpens and readies the inner psychic powers. Our success in sending telepathic messages can be facilitated by using this procedure immediately prior to the sending effort. If we are attempting to gain information about the future, this technique can pave the way for precognition to occur. In clairvoyance, this exercise stimulates imagery and allows relevant information to emerge.

PERIPHERAL GLOW PROCEDURE

Step 1 Select a small object, such as a piece of jewelry, a quartz crystal, or other shiny object. A crystal ball or lighted candle can be highly effective.

Step 2 Gaze at the object from a comfortable distance. Focus your full attention on the object and allow your mind to become passive by engaging no active thought.

Step 3 Slowly expand your peripheral vision as you continue to gaze at the object, gradually taking in as much of your surroundings as possible—above, below, and around the object.

Step 4 Allow your eyes to shift out of focus. At this point, you will note the peripheral glow effect, or a whitish radiance that bathes the object and spreads throughout your visual field.

Step 5 Slowly close your eyes and allow relaxation to permeate your body.

Step 6 With your eyes closed, give yourself the following general affirmation:

> *I am now at my psychic peak. My psychic powers are at my command.*

Step 7 Conclude with additional, more specific psychic empowering affirmations.

This procedure is especially useful in psychometry, a strategy in which a material object, such as an article of jewelry, is used to stimulate clairvoyance.

Relaxation strategies are important to psychic empowerment to alleviate tension and facilitate a state of physical balance and inner harmony. Balance and harmony are critical to psychic empowerment and personal well-being; and relaxation strategies are often complemented by highly specific techniques that focus directly on the mind's attunement systems to generate a state of empowerment readiness. A simple but effective technique designed to achieve inner balance and harmony is the Fingerpad Engagement Procedure. For this procedure, join the fingerpads of both hands in a praying-hands position, as empowering affirmations are presented:

> *I am surrounded by peace and tranquillity; I am*
> *protected and secure; I am infused with power.*

These general affirmations should be followed by specific affirmations that relate to personal concerns or even to global issues such as world peace.

A final strategy designed to reduce excessive stress while evoking a state of general empowerment is the Therapeutic Relaxation Induction Procedure (TRIP). Based on the PK principle of mind over body, or the capacity of the mind to deliberately influence bodily functions, the TRIP is a composite of many techniques including physical relaxation, empowering affirmations, mental imagery, and a unique attunement activation exercise.

THERAPEUTIC RELAXATION INDUCTION PROCEDURE

While seated, settle back and let yourself become as comfortable and relaxed as possible. Slow your breathing and develop a relaxed, rhythmic breathing pattern, taking a little longer to exhale. As you clear your mind, close your eyes and continue to focus your attention on your breathing. You are now ready to begin the TRIP.

Step 1   *Wrinkled Brow Rejuvenation Release.* Tighten the muscles in your forehead and between your eyes, then very slowly relax the muscles. Notice the relaxation as it spreads into the muscles of your forehead, around your eyes, over your face, and into your neck and shoulders. Feel the release of rejuvenating energy as it permeates your forehead and spreads downward.

Step 2   *Shoulder Lift*. Lift your shoulders and tighten the muscles as you hold them in the lift position. Slowly relax the muscles and let your shoulders return to normal, as you count from one to three. On the count of three, let the relaxation spread deeply into your chest and downward into your arms.

Step 3   *Finger Spread*. Spread the fingers of both hands and hold the spread position as you notice the tightness in the muscles of your hands and lower arms. Slowly relax the muscles in your fingers and hands, and allow the relaxation to soak into the joints and muscles of your hands and arms. Notice the pleasant tingling in your hands as the energy spreads right out through the tips of your fingers.

Step 4   *Abdominal Tuck*. Tuck in and tighten the muscles in your abdomen. Hold the tightened position for a few moments, then slowly relax the muscles. Notice the relaxation soaking into the muscles, going deeper and deeper into the pit of your stomach.

Step 5   *Knee Press*. Press your knees together very tightly. Hold them in the pressed position until you begin to tire, then slowly relax. You will notice the relaxation spreading above and below your knees. Let the relaxation go deeper and deeper into the muscles and joints of your legs.

Step 6 *Toe Lift.* For this step, you may wish to remove your shoes. Lift your toes and hold them in the lift position, as you notice the tension in your feet and ankles. Slowly relax your toes, allowing them to return to their normal position. Notice the relaxation in your ankles, feet, and right into the tips of your toes.

Step 7 *Attunement Activation.* Allow peaceful spontaneous imagery to flow gently in and out of your mind. Notice the color, movement, and detail of the imagery, but allow the images to come and go spontaneously.

After a few moments, select an image that seems right for you, and focus your full attention on it. Become so absorbed with the image that you lose yourself in the experience. Stay with the image until you have fully absorbed its energies.

Finally, let the imagery dissolve away until nothing remains. Your mind is emptied of all active thought. The systems of your being are neutralized, synchronized, and balanced inwardly and outwardly. Allow the attunement state to continue effortlessly.

Step 8 *Empowerment Affirmation.* Conclude by affirming:

> *I am now fully attuned inwardly and outwardly. My total being is infused with powerful, positive energy. I am empowered to activate my potentials and achieve my highest goals. The energies of growth are now unleashed to flow throughout my being.*

Mental Imagery

The third basic strategy considered essential to psychic empowerment is mental imagery. Imagery is important to empowerment, because it gives mental substance to verbal messages, while literally increasing the mind's capacity. In psychic empowerment, a mental picture is indeed worth a thousand words.

Like other cognitive abilities, imagery skills develop through practice and experience. As our imagery capacities unfold, other cognitive and psychic powers are enriched, and we become more attuned to the inner self, and increasingly aware of the richness of the world around us, with its beauty and its capacity to inspire and empower. As we develop our imagery powers, we acquire the language of the subconscious mind, and begin successfully to interact with subconsciousness, activating our deepest psychic potentials, and accessing knowledge which can enrich our lives.

Certain forms of sensory stimulation are known to promote empowering imagery. Listening to music can be both relaxing and empowering, because of its capacity to evoke imagery, and in some instances, to activate the mind's psychic faculties.

A more direct technique for evoking imagery and developing imagery skills is the Dream Recall Strategy. Dreams are often imagery messages from the subconscious mind. Practice in recalling those images can build imagery skills, while at the same time improving understanding of dreams. The Sequential Imagery Technique uses a similar strategy with a picture or scene; while the Regressive Imagery Procedure stimulates creativity through the recollection of a past experience. Finally, the Palm Memory Exercise concentrates the imagery skills on the palm of the hand, honing the ability to mentally recreate its full range of pattern and detail. These valuable exercises are outlined on the following pages.

DREAM RECALL STRATEGY

Step 1 Select a particularly vivid dream experience, perhaps a recurring dream.

Step 2 Mentally recreate the dream experience, paying careful attention to detail and dream action.

Step 3 Immerse yourself in the recall experience. If possible, become an active participant in the dream images.

Step 4 Allow the dream images to become increasingly vivid. Let yourself flow with the recall experience.

Step 5 Conclude the exercise with powerful, positive affirmations of your psychic potential.

SEQUENTIAL IMAGERY TECHNIQUE

Step 1 View a picture or scene, noting details such as shape, color, and texture.

Step 2 With your eyes closed, create a detailed mental image of the view.

Step 3 Once again, view the picture or scene as in step one, carefully noting its specific characteristics. Pay close attention to the features you did not include in your mental imagery of the view.

Step 4 With your eyes closed, mentally recreate the picture or scene, giving direct attention to the characteristics previously omitted.

Step 5 Repeat the procedure until you have mental command of the picture or scene in its entirety.

REGRESSIVE IMAGERY PROCEDURE

Step 1   Assume a relaxed, tranquil state of mind, and with your eyes closed, recall some past, rewarding experience in as much detail as possible. Experiences with nature are recommended, for example, a walk in a forest, a mountain climb, a summer thunderstorm, an inspiring sunrise, or a tranquil moonlit cove.

Step 2   Mentally recreate the experience and envision it as fully as possible. Notice movement, color, and sounds.

Step 3   Focus on your feelings, allowing yourself to relive the experience, interact with it, and absorb its peacefulness and tranquillity.

Step 4   Mentally travel back in time to an even earlier experience, perhaps your very earliest memory or a pleasant experience for which recall is sketchy. Project your awareness to that situation, and note in detail the characteristics of the experience.

Step 5   Enlarge your vision of the experience by filling in the missing parts and creating new pictures in your mind. Immerse yourself in the experience. Allow creative imagery to flow spontaneously, infusing your mind with the scene's peaceful tranquillity.

Step 6   Allow the imagery experience to run its course, and then, before opening your eyes, affirm:

> *I am now empowered to use my psychic resources and to develop them to their fullest. Whatever I choose to imagine can become my reality.*

PALM MEMORY EXERCISE

Step 1　View the palm of either hand or a photocopy of it. Particularly note the lines and their intensities, giving special attention to unusual patterns—triangles or crosses—formed by the lines.

Step 2　With your eyes closed, create a mental picture of your palm, with attention to details and characteristics.

Step 3　Again, view your palm, paying close attention to its unique features. Notice the characteristics you missed in the mental picture generated in step two.

Step 4　Close your eyes again and picture your palm in full and complete detail. Before opening your eyes, affirm:

> *The power of imagery is basic to my psychic growth. Through imagery, I am empowered to develop my full psychic potential.*

Profound insight often will emerge during ESP exercises that emphasize imagery, particularly images of movement. Precognitive awareness can be generated by relaxing the body and visualizing oneself being carried forward, possibly on a drifting cloud. A highly effective procedure using imagery of movement for expanding consciousness is the Stream of Consciousness. This procedure involves visual thinking, in which consciousness is experienced as a mountain stream that empties into the sea of universal consciousness.

STREAM OF CONSCIOUSNESS

A comfortable, reclining position is recommended, as the stream of consciousness is visualized, and related affirmations are given.

I am the stream of consciousness. Emerging from deep, mysterious caverns, I am flowing forward into the light of awareness and experience. Patiently and persistently, I advance toward the vast sea of understanding and expanded cosmic consciousness. At times tranquil and serene, I am momentarily content in my limited scope of awareness and my constricted range of knowledge; at other times, I am urgent and intense, demanding to increase my knowledge and to magnify my sphere of conscious experience.

I am the stream of consciousness. Settling into deep blue pools of introspection, languishing to reflect in the shade, I gather my resources before once again pressing forward, even more vigorously exploring, searching, discovering my inner being and the universe, forcefully unblocking barriers to my progress and growth.

I am the stream of consciousness. Slowly flowing among the towering trees of aspiration and weaving among the boulders of inner strength, I am cleansed, empowered, and invigorated by the positive energies of the universe and my own existence.

I am the stream of consciousness. Flowing into a sunlit valley of peaceful contentment, I am calm, confident, and secure as I advance steadily to join the illimitable sea of universal consciousness and cosmic oneness.

SUMMARY

As we increase our knowledge and understanding of ESP, we become more aware of the magnificent empowering potential of psychic phenomena. No longer is ESP seen as a mysterious, uncontrolled event, but rather as a purposeful, growth-oriented experience, with the capacity to enrich our lives with new insight and personal power.

Through mastery of ESP faculties—telepathy, precognition, and clairvoyance—we become empowered to achieve an advanced level of psychic awareness and self-fulfillment. If we are serious in our pursuit of psychic empowerment, we can settle for nothing less.

TELEPATHY

✌2✌

As a communication channel, telepathy is ESP in its most common form. Even non-psychic interactions often are accompanied by psychic elements that supplement and enrich both verbal and non-verbal communications. Perceptions and interpretations of expressed messages can be strongly influenced by the messenger's hidden motives, attitudes, and unexpressed thoughts, all of which can be psychically conveyed. An example of this concept is the inspirational message, in which complex, unexpressed content is transmitted psychically to move the audience. Persuasive or impassioned communications can include not only the expressed content, but also subtle psychic elements that can pave the way for attitude and behavioral change.

Some telepathic communications are exclusively psychic. Because they can occur independently of limiting sensory channels, telepathic messages conceivably can span the globe, or even be dispersed throughout the universe. Such psychic communications can be spontaneous or deliberate. Telepathic sending and receiving functions most often occur either simultaneously or in rapid sequence, but in some instances, the receiving function is initiated only after considerable delay.

Telepathy engages either the conscious or subconscious plane of awareness in both the sender and receiver. The typical telepathic message probably involves both planes to some extent, but the most highly active telepathic mechanisms seem to reside in the subconscious. In fact, our subconscious psychic functions are seldom, if ever, totally inactive. We become consciously aware of them only when we deliberately activate them, or when their spontaneous expressions are sufficiently intense as to demand our attention. This was illustrated by a teacher who, while attending an out-of-state seminar, experienced a strong, but unexplained urge to contact her husband. Upon reaching him by phone, she discovered that her mother had suddenly become ill. Her husband, having failed to reach his wife, had concentrated on the simple thought, "please call me," a message that evoked the teacher's immediate response.

In a similar instance, an architect discovered several essential documents her associate had inadvertently left behind, when he departed for an important out-of-town conference. She psychically engaged his attention by, in her words, "mentally commanding him to return to the office." Acting on an unexplained impulse, he immediately did so. His behavior was apparently activated by a simple telepathic communication designed to induce decisive, purposeful action—an example of telepathic empowerment at work.

Many telepathic messages have both informational and emotional content, each of which can be psychically perceived and acted upon by the receiver. Occasionally, however, the informational content will be lost in the psychic communication process, while the emotional content remains intact to elicit a commensurate change in the mood state of the receiver. A positive psychic message will often induce a positive mood state, even when the specific informational content of the message remains unknown to the receiver. It could be argued that information not consciously perceived, but nevertheless telepathically registered on a subconscious level, could produce commensurate changes in mood state as well; but it should be emphasized that a deliberately damaging, disempowering message typically generates a self-contained, enfeebling state within the sender alone. Destructive telepathic messages are damaging to the sender only, because external telepathic channels automatically close down when the message's motive is disempowerment. Positive telepathic messages tend to open the internal, as well as external psychic channels, the result being empowerment for both sender and receiver.

EXPLANATIONS OF TELEPATHY

Telepathy as a communication system has three essential elements: the sender, the receiver, and the communication medium. As already noted, the telepathic process can be conscious or subconscious as well as voluntary or involuntary. The sender in the communication system has two major functions: formulating the message in some appropriate encoded form, notably imagery, words, or symbols; and sending the encoded message. The receiver in the communication system also has two major functions: receiving the encoded message and decoding it. The remaining essential element in the system, the communication medium, is the psychically engaged minds of both sender and receiver.

In group telepathy, the essential elements remain unchanged: The collective psychic faculties of a sending group are organized to form and send the encoded message, while the collective psychic faculties of the receiving group function to receive and decode the message. In the group setting, the communication medium is the combined psychically engaged minds of the two groups.

One explanation of telepathy is the thought-as-energy perspective. This view holds that, once thought is generated, it exists as energy that can be transmitted and received as a thought-energy-transfer phenomenon between sender and receiver. At some point in the process, the receiving psychic mind deciphers the energy frequencies as meaningful messages.

Another view of telepathy speculates that the phenomenon involves a higher conscious or spiritual manifestation of the self. According to this view, the non-physical part of our being can transcend the purely physical or biological self to engage a telepathic interaction on a non-physical plane. Praying, mediumship, and psychic channeling are examples of potentially empowering telepathy on that plane. Empowering telepathy also occurs on a temporal or physical plane through the engagement of the sending and receiving faculties of our spiritual parts, but independent of any distant, external spiritual plane. This concept of telepathy suggests several empowering possibilities, including the capacity of our higher consciousness or spiritual side to telepathically interact within temporal and non-temporal dimensions; the empowering relevance of both temporal and non-temporal psychic interactions; the possibility of spiritual enlightenment through telepathic interactions with non-temporal or spiritual planes; and the survival of conscious and personal identity.

It is also possible that, among the brain's billions of cells and legions of faculties, there exists a psychic network that can engage an unlimited range of currently unexplained functions. Included are not only telepathy and supersensory awareness of the future and the world around us; but the power of biologically based functions, including thought processes, to influence matter, events, and minds.

A related view holds that cognitive psychic elements, including telepathy and other forms of ESP, exist within the cognitive structure of the brain. Like global or general intelligence that embodies multiple mental faculties, our psychic makeup includes a host of specific ESP and PK abilities which, along with other cognitive potentials, develop as the result of practice and experience. This perspective emphasizes the role of learning, memory, and reasoning and their importance to psychic growth. Psychic empowerment would thus require an organized instructional approach that recognizes individual differences in potentials, motivation, achievement levels, and rates of learning.

TELEPATHIC STRATEGIES

A cardinal principle of psychic empowerment holds that specific psychic faculties exist in a form that can be accessed, activated, and developed through appropriate instruction and guided learning experiences. The Strategic Telepathy Procedure (STP) is based on that principle. The procedure emphasizes objective analysis of the psychic experience, and a logical progression that invokes telepathy and promotes its development. STP is represented as follows:

1. *Practice.* Extensive practice is provided through the use of a variety of materials and techniques in a controlled instructional setting.

2. *Analysis.* Feedback, preferably immediate, facilitates the analysis of ESP performance to determine the variables associated with successful sending and receiving.

3. *Strategies.* Strategies based on scientific analysis are developed to activate telepathic sending and receiving.

4. *Validation.* Practice and further analysis of results refine procedures and improve telepathic skills.

This approach focuses on the personal and situational variables that could influence telepathy, particularly physical setting, mood states of sender and receiver, personality factors, and time of day. Interestingly, comparisons of the telepathic performances of men and women participating in the STP approach revealed that women typically performed better in the morning hours, whereas men typically performed better in the evening hours. Performance in the afternoon hours was found to be similar for men and women.

Based on analysis of the telepathic performances of individuals and groups practicing the STP approach, a procedure called the Composite Strategy was developed to facilitate telepathic sending and receiving. The procedure focuses on telepathy as a two-part phenomenon with clearly defined sending and receiving components. It identifies conducive conditions and specific procedures for activating each component. The Telepathic Activation Procedure (TAP) combines the components to enhance both sending and receiving skills.

COMPOSITE STRATEGY: TELEPATHIC SENDING

Step 1 Select the telepathic recipient and formulate the telepathic message.

Step 2 Become physically relaxed and mentally passive.

Step 3 Focus your full attention on the telepathic message. Simplify the message. If you use language, form simple sentences. Keep the content brief—complicated messages tend to become fragmented and distorted.

Step 4 With eyes closed, enrich the message with appropriate mental imagery. Try to use visual symbols. For example, the message, I love you, can be accompanied by the image of a heart with the word love superimposed.

Step 5 With eyes remaining closed, focus your full attention on the message and related imagery. Concentrate. Avoid any distraction that could weaken your concentration powers.

Step 6 As you concentrate, mentally or audibly articulate the message while continuing to engage the related mental imagery. Allow the articulated message and related imagery to merge as a powerful thought form.

Step 7 Envision the target. Release the thought form and mentally direct it to the envisioned target. Allow a few moments for thought transfer to occur. With experience, you will learn to sense when the message has been received.

Step 8 Close down your telepathic system by clearing your mind and relaxing your body.

We generally have no advance notice that we are the selected recipients of a telepathic communication. Our telepathic receiving under those circumstances is spontaneous, involving no receiving effort on our part. When we are aware of the sending effort, however, we can deliberately facilitate the receiving process.

COMPOSITE STRATEGY: TELEPATHIC RECEIVING

Step 1 Relax. Mentally scan your body, releasing all tension from your forehead to the tips of your toes. Develop a slow, rhythmic breathing pattern.

Step 2 With your eyes closed, extinguish all active thought. Clear your mind by imagining a mist or fog slowly moving in and closing off other images and thoughts.

Step 3 While your eyes remain closed, create a receptive state of mind. Allow new thoughts to emerge or new images to appear against a white background. Be patient. Allow sufficient time for the telepathic message to form.

Step 4   Upon receiving the message, close down the receiving system by relaxing your body and clearing your mind.

TELEPATHIC ACTIVATION PROCEDURE (TAP)

Step 1   For either sending or receiving, clear your mind while relaxing your body. An excellent mind-clearing and relaxation technique combines imagery of a clear, blue sky and the affirmation:

> *I am now becoming relaxed as my mind is cleared*
> *of all active thought.*

The clearing and relaxation process is further facilitated by breathing slowly and mentally scanning the body from the head down. Areas of tension are noted, and the muscles are progressively relaxed.

Step 2   For telepathic sending, formulate the message and related imagery. Visualize a vehicle, such as a beam of light or a transparent sphere, for transporting the thought message. Actively concentrate on the message and related imagery. Release the telepathic message to go forth to the envisioned target receiver.

Step 3   For telepathic receiving, maintain a mentally passive state and allow the thought messages and images to emerge into conscious awareness.

Both the Composite Strategy and the Telepathic Activation Procedure require practice, in which a variety of telepathic materials and messages is introduced. Although practice with aids such as ESP cards can be productive in exploring and developing our psychic capacities, marked improvements in psychic performance usually occur when highly interesting messages and meaningful materials are introduced into the practice sessions.

INNER-TELEPATHY

Telepathy is considered an *interpersonal* form of psychic communication between individuals or groups. It can be experienced, however, as an *intrapsychic phenomenon* in which the self, or more specifically, the separate parts of the self, function as sender and receiver. This extension of conventional telepathy reflects the power of our mental and physical subsystems to engage in an empowerment interaction that is fully autonomous and self-contained. Through inner-telepathy, empowering messages can be formulated and targeted to specific mental faculties and physical functions, resulting in a profound state of self-initiated psychic empowerment.

Inner-telepathy empowers us to assume command of the complex, ongoing interactions within the self. One of the most common examples of inner-telepathy is self-talk, through which we can generate positive thought messages that are subsequently dispersed, either generally throughout the self system, or specifically to selected inner targets. For example, we can build a positive state of self-esteem and personal well-being through self messages:

> I am a person of worth; I am capable, self-confi-
> dent, and secure; I am fully empowered.

When affirmed frequently and convincingly, these self-messages can generate a powerful, positive force within our physical and mental systems. When combined with more specific messages, they can empower us to achieve personal goals such as quitting smoking, losing weight, learning languages, improving memory, and succeeding in business. In fact, there are almost no limitations to the empowerment possibilities of inner-telepathy: It can activate dormant potentials or generate new ones. It can increase awareness and bring out desired change in the self. If practiced consistently, it can generate a continuous state of personal empowerment.

As with other forms of psychic phenomena, the empowering capacity of inner-telepathy can be expanded and its effectiveness magnified through relevant mental imagery. Given the vehicle of visualization, thoughts become powerful generators of growth. By giving substance to thoughts, imagery transports raw power to target destinations that include mental functions such as learning, creativity, and reasoning, and a host of biological processes, all of which respond to inner-telepathy. A state of mental and physical well-being can be psychically induced through positive thought and relevant imagery which unleash our inner wealth of empowering resources, while eradicating negative disempowering residue.

The capacity of the mind to generate thought messages and disperse them telepathically within the self is one of our most critical empowerment resources. However, that same capacity, if either misdirected or left unattended, can disempower both mind and body. Empowering thoughts are available to everyone and can be activated at any moment, letting us choose empowerment even in the most adverse or restrictive life situations.

Inner-telepathy can play a role in prompting the expression of other psychic faculties, particularly those of the subconscious mind. Clairvoyant and precognitive impressions are often experienced first in the subconscious, then intrapsychically conveyed to conscious awareness in either direct or disguised form. Inner-telepathy is the critical vehicle for the internal delivery of such awareness. Spontaneous phenomena such as slips of the tongue, pen, and sight, and repressed emotions that spill over into consciousness, could be explained as an inner form of telepathy. A military commander, acting on intuition alone, made a combat strategy decision that saved the lives of many soldiers. Such an action could be explained as a response to a detailed clairvoyant impression first experienced in subconsciousness, then delivered intratelepathically to consciousness, where it was experienced as an unexplained, but potentially empowering intuition.

We often observe the effects of intrapsychic communications in biofeedback settings, in which the influence of psychological factors on biological functions is carefully monitored. Changes in pulse rate, body temperature, blood pressure, and glandular functions, all of which were at one time thought to be autonomic and hence beyond the control of conscious intervention, are now known to respond to biofeedback techniques that utilize not only technology, but empowering mental imagery and self-affirmations. Among the benefits achieved are reduced stress, mastery of biological systems and organs, and enhanced wellness.

Another application of inner-telepathy concerns its efficacy in promoting creativity. An artist experienced a dramatic increase in creative ideas by envisioning a canvas upon which new works slowly unfolded as she affirmed, *My artistic potentials are now unleashed.* Similarly, a composer imagined a music staff upon which notes appeared as he affirmed, *My creative powers are now unfolding.* Such combinations of thought and imagery may generate a forceful message that is readily perceived and applied by the psychic mind to awaken dormant potential and creative ideas.

GLOBAL TELEPATHY

The human mind is the most powerful force in the universe. The more we explore its secrets, the more we come to appreciate its magnificent complexity and power. The mind is capable not only of thinking, reasoning, and remembering; it can also create, communicate, and empower. Conventional telepathy illustrates the power of the mind to interact psychically with others; intrapsychic telepathy illustrates the power of the mind to empower itself. Global Telepathy illustrates the power of the mind to bring about global change.

Global telepathy is based on the premise that we can engage mentally global interactions that, in turn, affect global conditions. Peace, for instance, can be seen as a product of positive human interactions engendered by thoughts of peace. It would follow that thoughts of peace on a global scale could literally *create* global peace. If individually we can shape our own destinies, collectively we can shape the destiny of the world.

SUMMARY

All too often we are out of touch with ourselves, with others, and with the universe. Telepathy can bridge the gaps that separate us, and expand our capacity to communicate and interact. It can bring forth personal insight and increase our understanding of others; and it can lift consciousness and empower us to achieve new levels of personal and global actualization.

PRECOGNITION

⹀3⹁

Precognition is a normal extension of our capacity for sensory awareness. Awareness of the past, present, and future exists on a time continuum that engages memory, sensation, anticipation, and finally precognition. Through memory, we can recall and reflect on the past. Through sensation, we experience the richness of the present. Through anticipation, we engage the future, setting goals and planning outcomes. Precognition accesses the future and delivers, on a need-to-know basis, realities that are yet to unfold. Through precognition and the consequent removal of time barriers, lives can be empowered, and awareness dramatically expanded.

Precognition is essential to psychic empowerment because it provides important information about the future that would otherwise be unavailable to us. Precognitive awareness can occur either as clear, concise messages, or as general, ill-defined impressions. In both forms, precognition functions independently of currently perceived conditions or known facts that could themselves give rise to predictions of consequences or outcomes. Forecasts should be considered psychic only to the degree that they do not depend on sensorially perceived information. Predictions of future economic trends, for example, are precognitive in nature only when they are not based solely on non-psychic knowledge, such as current economic trends or other economic growth indicators. Predictions concerning future behavior can be highly accurate based only on information about past behavior. The best single predictor of future performance of individuals, organizations, and even nations is past performance, or more specifically, immediate past performance. Highly accurate non-psychic predictions are often based exclusively on knowledge of the past. History does tend to repeat itself; and change often fits the cycles of previous change, thereby feeding predictions that require little or no psychic insight.

Many predictions are based on combinations of psychic and non-psychic knowledge. The expert's highly accurate hunch about the future is typically a product of a complex interaction of knowledge of current conditions, past trends, and influencing variables, along with analytical skills and psychic attentiveness. Political, economic, military, scientific, and social experts often disagree, even when given the same data. In complex situations, the critical determinant of predictive accuracy goes beyond the objective data and clearly includes expert analysis, interpretive skills, and possibly some psychic or intuitive insight.

Some very accurate predictions seem to be exclusively extrasensory in nature; that is, they appear to rely on no related sensory input. A British writer visiting northern Alabama paused while lecturing on the paranormal, and predicted a fire to be ignited by the open flame of a candle at a local nuclear power plant. Within a few weeks, a fire did indeed occur at the facility, and was attributed to the open flame of a candle. The prediction's specificity, and the fact that even the plant's existence was apparently unknown to the writer, suggests the exclusively psychic nature of her prediction. In another instance, a hunter's dream of his own accidental hunting injury proved all too accurate. The fact that the dream occurred before the hunting trip was planned, suggests a purely psychic awareness of the event.

Frequently, a seemingly unrelated situational cue will precipitate a spontaneous precognitive impression. The cue is often a "reality slip" that activates the mind's precognitive faculty. For instance, an employee in a chemical plant envisioned an explosion in the plant upon hearing thunder during an early afternoon storm. Later that day, the explosion occurred exactly as envisioned. Another example was reported by an accountant who, over lunch, mistook a voice from a nearby table to be that of his mother who lived in a distant city. The experience weighed upon his mind until later in the afternoon when he received a message that his mother had just suffered a light stroke. The reality slip as a precognitive signal was reported by a couple who, upon leaving their home, noticed a reflection of their car lights in a window that, at first, they mistook for a fire. Within a week, the house was destroyed by fire. These reality cues could be expressly designed to command our attention and to promote preparation for, or prevention of future occurrences.

Precognitive messages are occasionally antithetical in nature; that is, the precognitive material represents its opposite or direct contrast. A precognitive impression of failure can actually signify success. An impression of gain can signify loss. A woman who dreamed of discovering a valuable ring, instead lost such a ring the following day. A teenager's recurring dream of rear-ending a vehicle ceased only when his own vehicle was rear-ended. Fortunately, these antithetical precognitive messages are often accompanied by clues to their antithetical meanings. A trial attorney, for example, dreamed of a guilty verdict for his client. In the dream, however, the woman client was depicted as a man, a clear signal of the dream's true antithetical message, which later proved accurate—a not-guilty verdict for his client.

Like telepathy, precognition can include both thought and mood content. The mood content alone is the critical precursor of the impending event, with the mood state, except in antithesis, directly proportional to the event. Unexplained changes in mood state are particularly relevant, with an agitated, depressed state foretelling adversity or misfortune, and an elated, optimistic state predicting positive events. Several days prior to his tragic death in a plane crash, Ricky Nelson was reportedly despondent, a mood state considered highly uncharacteristic of the singer. Similarly, Clark Gable was reportedly depressed for several days before the accidental death of Carole Lombard. Formidable future events that will exact a heavy toll on our lives tend to signal their impending occurrence either to prepare us for the imminent misfortune or to help us avert it. An elated mood state, while forecasting good fortune, can enrich our lives with anticipation, as it increases the empowering value of the future event.

Consistently goal directed and potentially empowering, precognition may simply equip us with knowledge about what is to come: To be informed is to be empowered. Armed with this awareness, we become prepared to cope with the present and shape the future. Precognition empowers our lives in these ways:

- *Averting Misfortune.* Given advance awareness, we can avoid and, in some instances actually prevent the occurrence of adverse events.

- *Preparation.* Precognition enhances our ability to muster our resources to cope more effectively with formidable situations, and to build our resolve to meet the challenges of demanding, but potentially empowering, circumstances.

- *Enrichment.* Any degree of psychic awareness of the future expands the breadth and depth of our knowledge, while it enriches our lives by giving us a better understanding of the continuity of our experiences.

- *Problem Solving.* Precognition often delivers clear, quality solutions to specific problems. Through precognitive insight, we can enlarge our knowledge base and more accurately assess the consequences of our actions.

Precognition can involve matters of life and death significance, as was illustrated by a graduate student's detailed dream which may have saved the life of her husband, who was planning a business trip by car. Her dream identified the exact location of a multiple-vehicular accident on the mountain road her husband was to travel the following day. Awakening in the night, she shared the dream experience with her husband who, albeit skeptically, consented to approach the identified accident site with caution. Her husband called the next day to confirm the accuracy of his wife's dream. The prediction, he admitted, prevented his involvement in a serious accident that had just occurred on the winding road. Even when viewed with skepticism, precognition remains empowering.

A nurse's spontaneous precognitive impression also may have prevented a serious traffic accident. Upon nearing an intersection, she experienced a distinct impression of a car failing to yield the right of way. She applied her brakes only moments before a van suddenly appeared and skidded into her path.

Although reported instances of precognition involving adverse events are frequent, precognitive impressions typically concern ordinary, non-threatening life situations which are almost always enriched by the psychic experience.

One of our most common precognitive channels is the dream experience. The dream-state appears to function in a twofold precognitive capacity: First, it stimulates the mind's precognitive faculty; and second, it engages dream mechanisms to deliver precognitive information to conscious awareness, although frequently in disguised or symbolic form. As a precognitive channel, the dream state reflects an important source of precognitive knowledge: the subconscious mind creating within ourselves, a rich and complete system for expanding awareness and generating a state of precognitive empowerment.

Given the power of dream mechanisms to activate our precognitive faculties and deliver precognitive knowledge to consciousness, it would follow that advanced psychic strategies designed to initiate the precognitive dream experience could be particularly empowering. Such strategies have been developed and successfully implemented. The most productive approaches emphasize the role of pre-sleep suggestion and imagery, usually of being borne into the future. As sleep is delayed, precognitive affirmations are given and images are formed, such as a stream of consciousness flowing into the future or a beam of light connecting the present to future realities. A recommended technique for delaying sleep is a modified finger spread procedure, in which the fingers of either hand are held in a spread position as precognitive affirmations are presented:

> My dreams are a source of important knowledge
> and insight. I will understand my dream mes-
> sages and benefit from them. I can help the
> precognitive dream to occur. The future is now
> at my command.

The procedure is concluded by relaxing the fingers and affirming:

> I will now drift into deep, peaceful sleep.

A dream journal is an important component of any psychic strategy using the dream experience, because it can enhance recall and understanding of the dream message. Entries to the journal are made immediately upon awakening, to be reflected upon periodically during waking hours. The precognitive content of dreams will often become clear after a period of reflection, particularly when the dream's message is laden with symbolism or other disguises.

The dream journal is an important strategy for identifying the more complex "serial dream," in which sequential stages and future developments are presented. The precognitive serial dream was illustrated by a sociologist whose dreams predicted symbolically certain critical developments in his marriage. His dream journal described his first dream as simply, "I am running along the beach hand-in-hand with my wife." This dream assessed his current marital relationship, and established a baseline for subsequent dreams in the series. His second dream initiated the precognitive stage of the series: "Suddenly my wife is running very fast and I am unable to keep up with her." Two weeks following this dream, his wife, a fashion designer, received a career promotion that widened the gap in their incomes. In the third dream, he frantically searched for his wife, who had disappeared among large boulders on the beach. Following this dream, his wife was again promoted, this time to a position that required travel and long separations, exacting a heavy toll on the marriage. His fourth dream suggested an impending crisis: "We are in the ocean struggling to stay afloat. I reach out to her, but she drifts farther away. She calls for help, and I fight the waves to reach her." The fifth and final dream was a recurrence of the first dream, with the couple hand-in-hand, running playfully on the beach. This dream accurately predicted the eventual restoration of their marital relationship. The series of dreams correctly assessed stages in the relationship, while monitoring progress and predicting outcomes. Perhaps more importantly, the dream increased awareness of emerging needs in the relationship, and prompted a resolution of the marital crisis.

The precognitive dream often prepares us for future adversity. A clinical psychologist reported a recurring dream about red roses, which consistently occurred a few days before the death of a family member or friend. She viewed the dream, not as ill-omened, but rather as preparation for the event. In another instance, a business executive reported a recurring dream in which a fissure developed in the wall of his company's central administrative building. Although the dream continued over a period of several weeks, its precognitive significance—the future collapse of the company—

was not comprehended, and corrective action was not undertaken. When the business finally failed, the dream abruptly ceased.

Symbolism in precognitive dreams is not unusual, and in fact, can increase the empowering potential of the dream. Symbolism purposefully challenges us to unravel the dream's garment of disguise and discover its underlying empowering significance. Such involvement increases meaning and promotes acceptance of the precognitive message. We are likely to be empowered by experiences that challenge our imagination and demand investment of our energies. In that sense, dreams reflect a very basic, yet critical, condition for learning: the active involvement of the learner. To facilitate interpretation of the dream experience, a glossary of dream symbols is presented at the end of this book.

Like dreams, hypnosis and meditation facilitate precognition by probing the mind's psychic regions and actively stimulating precognitive channels. Frequently, precognitive insight will emerge spontaneously during hypnosis or meditation. More typically, direct suggestions designed to initiate precognition are required. The suggestions can be formulated to promote development of the precognitive faculty, or they can be tailored to target specific situations or outcomes. An interesting example of highly specific precognition was the lottery winner who envisioned the winning number during self-hypnosis.

PRECOGNITIVE STRATEGIES

Several step-by-step procedures have been designed specifically to stimulate precognitive awareness and promote development of the precognitive faculty. The Future Screen is a meditative approach that emphasizes the role of relaxation and imagery in exercising the precognitive faculty. The Doors Strategy emphasizes choice and self-determination. For practice in perfecting these skills, the Precognitive Review offers an exercise in envisioning future outcomes.

THE FUTURE SCREEN

Step 1   *Physical Relaxation.* With eyes closed, induce a physically relaxed state by slowing your breathing while mentally scanning your body from the head down, and allowing all muscles to become loose and limp.

Step 2   *Mental Passivity.* Clear your mind of all active thought. Allow a serene, passive mental state to emerge slowly.

Step 3   *Mental Screen.* Envision a blank screen upon which scenes of the future can be projected. At this stage, focus only on the blank screen.

Step 4   *Spontaneous Future Imagery.* Allow scenes from the future to appear spontaneously on the screen. Allow adequate time for meaningful images to form.

Step 5   *Selected Imagery.* To assume control over the future, generate images of desired developments or outcomes. Deliberately project them as clearly as possible upon the screen as images of the future.

Step 6   *Empowering Affirmations.* Conclude the procedure with positive affirmations that your precognitive powers are liberated and free to probe the future.

The Doors Procedure

Step 1   While in a relaxed, tranquil state, envision a wall with many doors and the word "future" boldly inscribed on the wall. Imagine doors of many colors and materials: gold, steel, wood, glass, silver, brass, and jade. Picture a word representing the future inscribed on each door: career, finances, relationships, family, and health; or more deeply personal inscriptions such as the names of people. They can be national or global in nature. Allow one door to remain without an inscription.

Step 2   Select a door and envision yourself opening it. Allow a panoramic view of the future to emerge. You may choose to step through the door and become an active participant in the unfolding events of the future.

Step 3   Select other doors and open them at will. The non-inscribed door is reserved for accessing information about the future concerning non-specified topics. The non-inscribed door is used to reveal future events such as natural catastrophes, political developments, and international incidents.

Step 4   Conclude the procedure with affirmations of your power to use precognitive knowledge responsibly to influence the future or to effectively accommodate unalterable future events.

PRECOGNITIVE REVIEW

Step 1   Identify a situation for which precognitive information would be useful.

Step 2   Realistically envision the prevailing situation, giving attention to specific details.

Step 3   Mentally enumerate the potential outcomes of the present situation. Identify as many alternatives as possible.

Step 4   Review the potential outcomes, turning them over one by one in your mind. Permit other outcomes to unfold mentally. Allow the process to continue until one outcome emerges as the strongest or most probable.

Step 5   Following a brief rest period in which the mind is cleared, repeat steps three and four, giving particular attention to any confirmation of the previous results.

Step 6   Continue the review process until a clear impression of the future unfolds. Document the results.

Aside from its usefulness as a practice exercise, Precognitive Review has been effective in generating awareness of specific future events related to a wide range of prevailing problems or conditions. Concerns regarding the future of personal relationships seem particularly appropriate for this procedure. College students have found this exercise useful as a source of information about graduate schools they will attend, geographic locations of their future employment, and career specialties they will pursue. It should be emphasized that Precognitive Review does not determine the future; it instead identifies the most probable future developments while, at the same time exercising the mind's precognitive mechanisms. Personal choice remains the major force shaping most future events.

SUMMARY

Precognition, whether spontaneous or induced, is consistently empowerment driven. In its spontaneous form, precognition is a reflection of our native capacity to experience the future independently of sensory input. In its induced form, precognition is an acquired skill developed through experience and practice of certain procedures and techniques. Through our precognitive skills, we can open many exciting doors into the future. Some of those doors may open upon destiny to reveal events that cannot be changed; but others will open upon possibilities and reveal strategies that can alter the future. Whatever the nature of the precognitive door, to be informed is to be empowered to plan, to avert, and to change.

Precognitive awareness empowers us to engage the present with enthusiasm, confident in our ability to shape the future and achieve our highest goals.

CLAIRVOYANCE

~4~

Clairvoyance is defined as the perception of tangible objects, current events, or existing conditions not present to the senses, but nevertheless having objective reality. Unlike telepathy, clairvoyance functions independently of another mind, except in instances of collective clairvoyance, in which the clairvoyant faculties of two or more persons are combined to preternaturally perceive existing realities. Unlike sensory perception, clairvoyance requires no stimulation of sensory mechanisms, and is not subject to the limitations of conventional sensory experience.

Clairvoyance is quite possibly the most intricate and advanced form of ESP. It reflects the wondrous capacity of the human mind to expand its own field of awareness to encompass unbounded realities. Clairvoyance is the *ne plus ultra* of psychic experience. It can bring the earth into panoramic view, and link us to the infinite expanse of the universe. Through clairvoyant enhancement, the terrain of the cosmos can become a vivid and exciting playground for the psychic mind.

The underlying dynamics of clairvoyance are complex and not yet fully understood. They appear to be distinctly unlike those of either telepathy or precognition. In the absence of the influence of another mind, the sources of clairvoyant knowledge must lie within the self or in some external condition or energy source. The bulk of clairvoyant insight probably engages both sources, but we "see through a glass darkly" in our efforts to explain this remarkable and potentially empowering phenomenon.

The fact that tangible objects are often instrumental in initiating clairvoyance suggests that it may not be altogether self-contained. Objects such as the crystal ball are often used to facilitate clairvoyance and access new psychic knowledge. Beyond simply providing the point of focus often considered critical to many psychic functions, some tangible objects seem to provide the conditions for mental interactions that extend beyond inner processes alone. The mind becomes engaged in a complex exchange which can generate profound psychic insight.

Occasionally, the object spontaneously invokes the clairvoyant faculty, and functions as the essential channel for the clairvoyant message. A mother, whose son was injured in a random, late night shooting in a distant city, awakened at the exact hour of the shooting to the sound of a trophy crashing to the floor in her son's vacant bedroom. She immediately sensed danger involving her son. In another instance, a student, distraught over the death of her grandmother, reported a dream in which her grandmother appeared with a yellow rose and the message, "This rose is especially for you. I send it with happiness and love." A few days later, she received a beautiful yellow rose from her grandmother's sister with the message, "This rose is especially for you. I send it with happiness and love." Although the dream experience could be interpreted as precognitive, the student saw it as a clear clairvoyant manifestation of her grandmother's successful transition, which was confirmed by the gift of the yellow rose.

Specific clairvoyant data is often accessed through the deliberate use of related physical objects. Psychometry is the clairvoyant application of relevant objects to gain highly specific psychic information. A clairvoyant, for instance, located a teen runaway through information gained by holding the teen's bracelet. Psychometry also includes the clairvoyant use of non-personal but relevant aids to locate missing articles. A psychometry study group used a map of a shopping mall to locate a lost ring. A floor plan provided the framework required by another study group to locate a valuable antique brooch. The combined impressions of the group pinpointed the brooch's exact location: inside an old baby shoe stored in the bottom drawer of a bedroom chest.

Frequently, the dream experience provides the channel for clairvoyant knowledge. Clairvoyant insight, like precognitive awareness, often seems to reside in the subconscious. Dream mechanisms logically could promote a subconscious transfer of information to conscious awareness. Common among the dream's clairvoyant functions is the delivery of information concerning urgent situations. A building contractor's dream, for instance, identified a critical error in the blueprints of a building under construction. An attorney's dream identified the exact location of an important legal document which had been lost. Unexplained synchronicity is sometimes observed in clairvoyant dreams, particularly among individuals who are closely associated or related. Two brothers, eighteen and twenty-one years of age, reported simultaneously dreaming of their parents' involvement in a serious train accident. Their dreams, according to their report, vividly detailed the accident at the exact time of the event.

The clairvoyant dream will often provide clues concerning its psychic significance. Among frequently reported clues are the immediate awakening of the sleeping subject upon conclusion of the dream, the vivid physical sensations accompanying the dream experience, and the convincing, often urgent nature of the dream. The clairvoyant dream can generate a strong motivational state to either act upon the dream or to investigate its psychic significance.

Clairvoyant dreams, like precognitive dreams, have been known to occur in a series that guides the dreamer, often symbolically, and monitors the dreamer's progress. This form of clairvoyant dreaming is usually characterized by a central theme and a succession of related events. Transitional life situations and personal crises tend to precipitate the serial clairvoyant dream. Its goal is empowerment through personal insight. Once recognized and understood, such dreams can provide important therapeutic support and guide the growth or recovery process. This was illustrated by a college student who was undergoing therapy to resolve the trauma of sexual abuse during childhood. His series of clairvoyant dreams provided a weathervane of his progress from social withdrawal to rewarding interpersonal relationships. The dreams further provided the essential support required for overcoming the painful trauma. The serial clairvoyant dream is yet another manifestation of the skilled therapist existing within each of us. Our inner-therapist, like our inner-teacher, probes our world of experience with persistence and a singular purpose: the full empowerment of the self.

CLAIRVOYANT STRATEGIES

The clairvoyant faculty frequently engages our most advanced non-psychic faculties, including our creative imagery powers. These powers can translate clairvoyant impressions into images that depict meaningful realities. Not surprisingly then, exercises designed to develop clairvoyant skills are usually more effective when they emphasize activities that promote creative imagery, such as sculpting, drawing, painting, and other forms of creative work or play.

Meditation exercises that focus on creative imagery seem particularly conducive to clairvoyant empowerment. The third eye, a chakra thought to be connected to the pituitary gland and associated with clairvoyance, appears particularly responsive to meditation strategies that engage the mind's imagery powers. The following exercise was specifically designed to develop that faculty.

THE THIRD EYE EXERCISE

Step 1   Induce a relaxed state using such techniques as body scan, relaxing imagery, and slowed breathing.

Step 2   With eyes closed, envision a smooth, glass-like plane void of disruptive structures.

Step 3   Imagine a myriad of glowing, geometric structures—spheres, obelisks, cubes, pyramids—as they rise above the plane.

Step 4   Focus on the structures and allow images to emerge as if projected on their surfaces.

Step 5   From among the various images, select a particularly relevant one and allow a progressive, spontaneous unfolding of new images.

Step 6   Mentally create a dominant structure to function as a clairvoyant screen, and project upon it the critical elements of a current situation for which additional information is sought. Allow new information to unfold on the screen as clairvoyant images.

Step 7   Conclude the exercise with positive affirmations of clairvoyant empowerment.

This exercise has demonstrated particular usefulness in locating missing items, as illustrated by a college student who used the procedure to find a lost sorority pin. During step six of the exercise, she erected a mental pyramid on the plane and projected an image of the pin on its surface. Almost instantly, the pin became surrounded by images that revealed its exact location: inside a candy tin stored in a desk. In a more dramatic application, a twin, who was separated from her sister in childhood, projected the image of her sister on a sphere she had mentally erected on the plane. A map of Canada first appeared on the sphere, then a close-up of British Columbia, and finally a close-up of Vancouver. She eventually reunited with her sister, who had been living in Vancouver for more than twenty years.

Certain strategies for inducing the precognitive dream can be readily adapted to accommodate clairvoyant dreaming. The finger spread procedure, can be applied to delay sleep while clairvoyant autosuggestions are presented. Affirmations such as those that follow are usually sufficient to promote clairvoyant dreaming.

> *My clairvoyant powers will be activated as I sleep. My inner psychic powers will generate the insight I need as I sleep.*

These general affirmations can be supplemented with specific statements to access solutions and detailed clairvoyant information.

Clairvoyance, like other forms of ESP, improves with practice. Practice in meditation designed to enhance the mind's creative capacities is particularly valuable, because it builds the basic skills underlying not only clairvoyance, but many other psychic faculties as well. Our surroundings also provide practice opportunities for developing clairvoyant skills. Effective activities involve familiar materials and everyday situations. Excellent practice exercises include guessing the time before checking, pulling a book from a shelf and guessing its total number of pages, and guessing the amount of change in your pocket or purse. With practice, these simple activities can strengthen clairvoyant skills and the capacity to initiate clairvoyance at will.

Occasionally clairvoyant data are revealed rather amusingly in reverse or other disguised form. In one instance of clairvoyant reversal, the 382 total pages of a book were clairvoyantly discerned as 283 pages. In a group practice session, the name "Peru," written on a concealed card, was clairvoyantly perceived by the group as "Urep," clearly a psychic impression in reverse form, but mistakenly interpreted as signifying Europe.

SUMMARY

Clairvoyance is our claim to oneness with the world in the here and now. Expanded awareness through clairvoyance empowers us with an unlimited width, breadth, and depth of knowledge, which reveals what we otherwise cannot see, as it enriches our lives with new ideas and creative solutions. Equally important as these profound revelations are the simple joys of the clairvoyant experience itself, such as that felt in the discovery of a lost possession or the sudden "Ah ha!" of clairvoyant insight.

Whatever the nature of its expression, clairvoyance is empowerment in highly practical form: It can provide the critical information we need to solve our most pressing problems and achieve our loftiest goals. Clairvoyance is so basic to the empowered life that, without it, we often grope in darkness, out of touch with critical sources of psychic enlightenment.

PSYCHOKINESIS

∽5∽

Nowhere is the power of the mind more dramatically evident than in Psychokinesis (PK). The term "mind," as applied to PK empowerment, is viewed holistically, and includes the sources, processes, and products of thinking, feeling, perceiving, and being. Although PK is considered primarily a mental phenomenon, the psychic empowerment perspective expands the scope of PK to embrace its capacity to command physiological functions in autonomic biological systems.

PK, also known as telekinesis, is the power of the mind to influence objects, events, and processes in the apparent absence of intervening physical energy or instrumentation. Within this definition of PK is the assumed capacity of the mind to generate and target energy to influence not only external matter and conditions, but also internal physiology, including body tissue and organ functions. The potential empowerment applications of PK thus include almost unlimited possibilities for psychic intervention into spatially distant realities, as well as the internal physical environment, and possibly even physical behavior.

Like other psychic phenomena, PK can be spontaneous or deliberate. We encounter many situations that activate PK to influence events around us. In emergencies involving near-accidents, such as a skidding automobile, we may attempt, both physically and mentally, to bring the situation under control. Even as passengers, we tend to catch our breath and tense our muscles, rather than passively await a collision. We may press the floorboard—our substitute for brakes—as we mentally attempt to slow the skidding vehicle. From the non-psychic perspective, these reactions are explained simply as responses to perceived danger; but psychically, these spontaneous reactions could reflect an innate, but dormant, capacity to intervene mentally into the physical world of matter and movement. We have probably all accidentally dropped a valuable, fragile object, such as an expensive vase, and found ourselves reacting both physically and mentally in an effort to slow the fall, and to prevent or minimize damage to the object. Incredibly, in some instances, it actually seems effective. The fragile object may bounce instead of shatter. Such spontaneous manifestations of PK suggest a valuable empowerment possibility: the ability of sheer mind power to influence matter and movement.

On a larger scale, the empowerment potential of PK is particularly evident in competitive sports events, in which the mental states of participants and spectators appear to influence the physical performance of athletes. A positive state of mind and a strong anticipation of success assert a powerful influence in any performance situation. In fact, the decisive factors determining success or failure are often psychological. In team events, the cumulative psychic energies of the team can create a force that heightens its physical capacities and sharpens its skills. Likewise, the empowerment effects of spectators who pull for a team are decisive factors that can shift the balance and determine which team wins. Usually, the larger the spectator support group and the more focused its energies, the greater its PK empowering effect, particularly in sports activities requiring a high degree of concentration and precision. Conversely, negative energy directed against a team or another person can return like a boomerang to disempower the sender.

In complex activities such as gymnastics, karate, ballet, and figure skating, the mental state of the performer can be the critical factor influencing performance. The addition of empowering imagery and success affirmations can accelerate learning and improve performance. The self-confidence and fine-tuning required for a perfect performance involve a mind-over-body state, and a heightened awareness of the smooth emergence of mental power, conditions recognized as essential by most performing artists.

PK, as the capacity of the mind to influence matter and physical events, is usually a goal-oriented phenomenon with highly practical empowering consequences. A teacher reportedly used PK to slow her fall down a flight of stairs, thereby preventing injury. Upon falling, she caught her breath and thought, "Slow motion." She recalled, "I felt myself flowing with the fall until I firmly said, 'Stop!' I escaped the fall without even a bruise." In a similar instance, an engineer, who had just purchased a car, experienced a PK event that may have saved his life. While attempting to negotiate a curve on an unfamiliar road, he lost control of the car as it began to skid toward a railing. With his foot on the brake, the car continued out of control until finally he commanded the car to stop. It stopped immediately, as if in direct response to his command. In another instance, a student with a history of migraine headaches discovered, while enrolled in a biofeedback class, that he could control the headaches by physically relaxing and deliberately elevating the temperature of his fingers. Basic to biofeedback is the concept of mind-over-body, or the capacity of mental processes to alter physical functions. These examples reflect the extensive range of the empowering possibilities of PK.

STAGES OF A PK EVENT

Typically, PK occurs as a spontaneous, goal-driven phenomenon. When we consider the many manifestations of PK, its existence and empowering potential become increasingly evident. PK could be considered an on-going mental phenomenon, constantly influencing both internal and external physical realities. Even though this complex interaction is far from fully understood, there are certain progressive stages that appear to characterize the typical PK event.

Alert Stage

At this stage, the PK potential is mentally alerted and placed in a state of empowerment readiness. In spontaneous situations, this process is usually instant and effortless; whereas in the experimental situation, it is deliberate. Three conditions seem conducive to alerting the PK potential: formulation of clear objectives; envisioning of desired results; and positive expectations of success. The alert stage also requires self-confidence and resolution to stimulate PK. A positive mental state activates alertness and increases PK powers. Doubt is disempowering, because it nullifies the alert stage and dilutes the PK potential.

Centering Stage

At this stage, PK energies are generated either spontaneously or through concentration, and then mentally assembled into an appropriate image, such as a nucleus of energy or a surrounding glow.

Focusing Stage

The centered energies are mentally aimed at the target. At this stage, continued concentration is critical to voluntarily activate the PK potential. The mind is cleared of distractions and, for an unseen target, the eyes are closed to form a clear image of the target.

Releasing Stage

In this final stage, the focused energies are mentally released. For voluntarily induced PK, strong affirmations or commands are crucial at this stage. For unseen targets, images of desired effects are generated as PK commands are presented. Such direct commands as move, bend, stop, and where tissue or bone are involved, repair, make whole, or heal are effective empowering commands.

PK STRATEGIES

Practice strategies that exercise the PK potential also accelerate its development. Among the simplest exercises is the PK Bombardment Drill, a coin-flipping procedure consisting of the following:

PK BOMBARDMENT DRILL

Step 1   Clear your mind, and with your eyes closed, envision the desired outcome (head or tail) prior to each coin toss. Affirm:

> *I will influence the fall of this coin.*

Step 2   Toss the coin and assume firm control by focusing your energies on it. Bombard the coin with energy, images, and verbal commands of the desired outcome.

Step 3   Continue bombarding the coin until it comes to rest.

The PK Bombardment Drill, along with most other PK practice exercises—tossing dice or attempting to bring a pendulum into motion—can be readily adapted to group PK. Group PK is based on the premise that the combined PK faculties of a group can be organized to produce a synergistic PK effect. Critical to group PK are a positive and cooperative group interaction, consensus of purpose within the group, and a fusion of the group's psychic energies. Group participation in goal-setting and problem-solving can produce necessary group cohesiveness and teamwork skills prior to the PK activity.

PK AND WELLNESS

Observed instances of PK in both controlled settings and real-life situations suggest a psychic concept with exciting empowerment implications: Given the capacity to influence objects and events external to the self, we might assume the ability to mentally influence the complex inner processes and mechanisms essential to our physical and mental well-being.

The capacity of mental factors to influence the physical body suggests profound empowering possibilities. Unfortunately, that same capacity also suggests potentially disempowering consequences. Many physical illnesses are associated with disempowering stress that chips away at our physical systems. Given time, excessive stress leads to serious tissue damage and organ dysfunction. Because they are initiated or exacerbated by psychological factors, these disorders are diagnostically related to psychological factors affecting physical conditions. Common examples are tension headache, migraine headache, arrhythmia, neurodermatitis, and certain immune deficiencies. Almost every major category of disease can, in fact, be affected by psychological factors.

If disempowering mental factors can contribute to the initiation or exacerbation of a physical condition, it would follow that the alleviation of stress and disempowering mental states could promote tissue repair and normal organ function. Even more exciting is the possibility of active intervention in preventing illness and promoting mental and physical well-being.

The mind and body are in a state of constant interaction. Wellness strategies are designed to tap into that interaction and alter it to meet the goals of wellness. The psychic wellness concept is based on the premise that inner resources exist in a form that can be psychically accessed and distributed throughout the physical body, if we recognize our inner wellness potential and are willing to unleash our inner wellness energies.

The Wellness Activation Strategy was designed to promote a mental state conducive to wellness, and to activate those psychic potentials, particularly PK, that can generate and distribute wellness energies throughout the physical body. Critical elements in the strategy are positive affirmations of personal well-being accompanied by related wellness imagery. The strategy requires a relaxed state and consists of six essential steps. Each step as presented below can be altered to include additional affirmations to meet specific wellness needs.

WELLNESS ACTIVATION STRATEGY

Step 1   With eyes closed, slow your breathing and mentally scan your body as you relax. Begin by affirming:

> *I am day by day becoming a more confident, secure person. I am becoming increasingly aware of my inner potential for wellness and well-being. The powers of my conscious mind are now merging with the hidden energies deep in my subconscious mind to influence my total being with vibrant health. As I interact with the innermost part of my being, I am empowered with positive energy and new vigor.*

Step 2 With your eyes remaining closed, envision a glowing wellness core as an empowerment generator situated in your body's central or solar plexus region. Affirm:

> *My potential for wellness is intensifying, becoming centered in the luminous core of my being. I am now fully energized with the glow of wellness.*

Step 3 Further activate the wellness core by envisioning an expansive, luminous field of energy surrounding the core, as you present the affirmation:

> *The empowering wellness core in the innermost part of my being is now saturated with brilliant energy, pulsating with potential as its wellness capacity reaches its peak. I am now prepared to absorb powerful wellness energy throughout my being.*

Step 4 Mentally disperse wellness energies as rays of light throughout your body. Image your body enveloped in a glowing aura of wellness as you present this affirmation:

> *My empowerment potential for wellness in now fully activated. The central, brilliant core of wellness is now radiating powerful wellness energies throughout my total being. My mind and body are absorbing soothing, invigorating, rejuvenating wellness. The glow of wellness now envelops my total body as an aura of health and vitality.*

Step 5 Imagine your circulatory system as a conveyor of powerful wellness energy. Permeate the organs and systems of your body with the glow of wellness. Affirm:

*I now direct wellness to each system, organ, and
function of my body, strengthening and fortify-
ing them with powerful energy.*

Step 6 Conclude the exercise with the affirmation:

*I am now fully enveloped with wellness energy. I
can activate, as needed, my inner resources to
promote wellness and well-being. My life is
enriched with positive, creative energy. By imag-
ing the luminous core of wellness within, I am
empowered to disperse wellness throughout my
body and being.*

The application of PK to wellness is a promising area of psychic
empowerment. To be empowered, we must understand the relevance of PK to wellness, because to limit PK to external conditions
alone is contradictory and potentially disempowering.

PK AND REJUVENATION

Possibly no human function is more complex than aging. Physical,
social, cultural, environmental, psychological, and psychical factors
all interact as influences to aging; and, within that intricate system,
the empowered self can emerge to assume a central role with the
capacity to intervene and direct the interaction. The self can retain
power to alter its own systems and functions, including the aging
process. The application of PK to aging suggests a state of empowered control over physiology, including systems typically considered
autonomous. Through the appropriate direction of our inner PK
faculty, we can alter crucial aging variables and activate our inner

rejuvenating potentials, thus restoring the natural flow of youthful energy and, in some instances, literally reversing the aging process.

The term "rejuvenation," as used in psychic self-empowerment, implies the deliberate restoration of youth and vigor through self-intervention into the aging process. Psychic rejuvenation recognizes the aging effects of an array of negative mental states, among them, anxiety, depression, hostility, and insecurity. Even more importantly, psychic rejuvenation emphasizes the constructive effects of *positive* mental states, along with the empowering capacity of positive states to eliminate their negative opposites. Love, for example, is one of the most empowering rejuvenation elements known. When present in the psyche, it neutralizes hate, its negative counterpart that is physically and mentally destructive and disempowering. Such positive states as self-confidence, self-esteem, self-acceptance, and a sense of personal adequacy are empowering and rejuvenating. They inject rejuvenating energies into the self system, eradicating those disempowering states which contribute to aging.

Our application of PK to rejuvenation recognizes three important principles:

1. Aging is primarily a physical phenomenon. Any alteration of aging must engage the mind's power to influence physiology.

2. Aging is a complex process with many determinants. Some of those determinants, such as genetic factors or biological predispositions, resist intervention and direct alteration. Others, being psychosocial, are susceptible to the empowered self, allowing their functions to be altered or extinguished altogether. Equally important, new functions affecting aging can be introduced into the self system.

3. Any alteration of the psychosocial determinants of aging will invariably alter the underlying physiology of aging.

Together, these principles suggest several profound empowerment possibilities. First, our physical processes, including aging, are not beyond the reach of the empowered self. When we introduce positive elements conducive to rejuvenation, the physical aging process is altered. Dormant rejuvenating forces already existing within the self can be accessed and activated to intervene directly into the physical aging process; and weakened rejuvenating elements can be strengthened through the application of this strategy. Finally, the negative energies and interactions underlying accelerated aging can be extinguished.

The extension of PK to include rejuvenation suggests that psychic strategies could evoke rejuvenation changes, not only in biological functions, but in outward physical appearance. A procedure called Rejuvenation PK activates the body's rejuvenation potentials through a process that unblocks the flow of inner rejuvenating energies. This procedure is similar to PK wellness strategies in that it involves empowering imagery and affirmations. Through Rejuvenation PK, physical functions, including those considered autonomic or involuntary, are linked to mental functions in a positive rejuvenating interaction. The results are actual and observable changes in the physical body.

REJUVENATION PK

Step 1   *Relaxation.* Physical relaxation sets the stage for PK intervention into the body's many functions. A progressive, cognitive relaxation procedure in which breathing is slowed and muscles are allowed to relax from the forehead downward is recommended, followed by the affirmation:

I am now in full charge of my body. I am capable of influencing every function, mental and physical. All the rejuvenating energies of my being are now at my command.

Step 2   *Stress Expiation.* Relaxation procedures are intended to reduce stress; but even when stress is reduced, certain residual effects tend to linger. The goals of stress expiation are first, to extinguish all residual effects of stress, and second, to infuse the physical body with positive, rejuvenating energy. To achieve these goals, major systems and organs are imaged and mentally energized. (The imagery process is facilitated if the subject has some knowledge of human physiology and the functions of various physical systems.) Energizing the body's systems and organs is accomplished by centering full awareness on various body regions and mentally bathing them with glowing energy, presenting the affirmations:

Youthful, invigorating energy is now flowing throughout my body. All organs, systems, and functions are now revitalized. The wear-and-tear of stress is now replaced by the flow of youth and vigor.

Step 3   *Balance.* The goal of this step is to establish a state of mental and physical equilibrium. With the body physically relaxed and the effects of stress expiated, an empowering state of full balance is possible through the Fingerpad Engagement Procedure. Designed to balance left- and right-brain functions, the procedure is effective in attuning the mind and body, a condition considered essential to rejuvenation. To implement this procedure, bring the tips of your fingers together; then with the fingerpads in a comfortable contact position and your eyes closed, imagine your hands as antennae for your brain. Imagine your left brain actively generating positive energy, which flows into your right hand as the extension of that hemisphere. Next, imagine your right brain actively generating positive energy, which flows into your left hand as the extension of that hemisphere. Allow the energies flowing into your hands and merging at your fingertips to engage in a powerful exchange that balances your mental and physical systems. After a few moments, disengage your fingerpads and allow your hands to relax, palm sides up. Conclude with the affirmation:

My total being is now fully balanced and infused with powerful rejuvenating energy. The energies of youth are now unleashed to flow throughout my being. I am completely attuned within myself and with the world.

Note that, although left- or right-hemisphere dominance is considered normal, balancing the cognitive and physical energies between the two hemispheres increases the efficiency of both, without affecting their functional asymmetry.

Step 4 *PK Illumination.* This is the final and most critical step in Rejuvenation PK. In this step, the rejuvenation process reaches its peak. PK illumination is initiated by viewing a picture of yourself taken at your youthful prime. (If no picture is available, you can create one mentally.) Study the picture, carefully noting the youthfulness in your eyes. Now close your eyes and imagine yourself at your peak of youth standing before a full-length mirror. Study your eyes in the mirror and observe the youthful gleam. Next, surround your entire body with a glow of energy, then think of your favorite color and allow the glow to take on that color. Finally, while breathing slowly and rhythmically, soak in the colorful rejuvenating glow enveloping your body. Conclude with the affirmation:

My inner powers of rejuvenation are now being unleashed to permeate my total being with the glow of youth and vigor. Every system within is now being revitalized with the infusion of rejuvenating power. Tired, worn tissue is being fortified with the energies of youth. Every function of my body is now fully infused as sparkling, youthful energy is absorbed into every cell and fiber. Surrounded by a colorful aura of rejuvenating energy, I am now secure in the present, bathed in vitality and the glow of youth. My inner rejuvenating powers are fully and completely unleashed to flow freely throughout my total being. Each day, my mind and body will absorb the abundance of youthful energy that is constantly being unleashed within my being. Whenever I envision myself enveloped with the colorful glow of radiant energy, I will immediately become invigorated and fully empowered.

A small, self-adhesive star of appropriate color can be strategically situated—on a mirror, computer, or TV, for instance—as a cue to periodically activate the inner flow of rejuvenating energy.

The complete PK Rejuvenation procedure can be practiced daily, or as often as desired, to maximize its rejuvenating effects. Instantly infuse the mind and body with rejuvenation at frequent intervals throughout the day, by using the colored star as a cue to recreate the imagery of the colorful glow of energy. With practice, the imagery and affirmation process becomes a natural, spontaneous, and continuous function of the psychically empowered self.

Together, positive affirmations, empowering imagery, and PK form a powerful three-component system of wellness and rejuvenation. In that system, PK assumes a critical role as the essential vehicle for physical change.

SUMMARY

PK is psychic empowerment in its most material form. It provides dramatic evidence of the power of the mind to intervene into the physical world of matter and movement. As an empowering phenomenon, PK meets the ultimate test of psychic empowerment: it can enrich our lives and bring forth empowering change. Whether to promote wellness, stimulate healing, activate rejuvenation, or simply to influence external conditions or events, the PK faculty spontaneously maintains a state of readiness which is responsive to our personal and situational needs. We can enrich the empowering ability of this important faculty through practice and experience, the result being an abundance of positive energy which can be maintained and expended as needed.

PART TWO

The Tools of
Psychic Empowerment

AN OVERVIEW

6

Psychic phenomena do not always lend themselves to direct activation. We often seek indirect means to access and stimulate our inner psychic functions. These methods can include psychic empowering strategies that involve altered states—hypnosis, self-hypnosis, meditation, and dreams—or psychic tools, which typically are material objects purposefully applied to connect us to sources of psychic power within the self. We call the study of these tools and the strategies associated with them "objectology." Among the frequently used tools in objectology are the familiar crystal ball, the pendulum, dowsing rods, the pyramid, and various forms of ESP cards.

It is important to note that psychic empowerment tools are valuable, not only in stimulating psychic functions, but also as research tools for exploring and better understanding the world of psychic phenomena. Through the use of tangible objects, we can assemble observational data that can be statistically analyzed for significance and relevance to the psychic experience. Dowsing rods, for example, can yield specific data regarding natural subterranean resources which can be analyzed for accuracy. Likewise, the pendulum can provide a wealth of psychic data in a quantified form that can be treated statistically. ESP cards are often used by researchers to determine the very presence of psychic faculties, and thus provide comparisons of psychic abilities among individuals. Many of our conclusions concerning the nature of psychic phenomena are based on the results of studies using tangible objects under controlled, scientific conditions.

Paralleling the use of objects in purposeful research is the spontaneous, though often unexplained role they play in real-life situations. Like the lyricist's grandfather's clock that "stopped short, never to run again when the old man died," some objects appear almost to have a mind—or an energy—of their own. They seem to function as mediators that manifest critical psychic information, particularly concerning individuals with whom they are closely associated. An attorney reported that a bronze figure—a gift from his grandson—toppled mysteriously from a bookcase in his office at the very moment his grandson was seriously injured in a traffic accident. A student reported that a plant—a birthday gift from her mother—fell from its place over a kitchen sink at the exact moment her mother suffered a heart attack. Although we could dismiss these phenomena as simply chance occurrences, the high frequency of such events illustrates an interesting possibility: In the psychic realm, tangible objects can spontaneously, yet purposefully, deliver critical psychic information.

The use of objects as communication tools in our daily lives is not uncommon. Trophies, certificates, and awards not only recognize accomplishments, they also satisfy certain ego or status needs. Frequently, objects are used deliberately to influence the perceptions of others or to compensate for our own felt weaknesses. For instance, a highly successful contractor, from a somewhat impoverished background, occupies an unusually luxurious and pretentious office that, he observes, "leaves no doubt about my success." In another vein, a businessperson, previously convicted of embezzlement, conspicuously displays a Bible in his office and on the dashboard of his car because, "It sends a good message." An executive, who was a high-school dropout, prominently places the works of Shakespeare and Greek classics on the shelves in his office. Similarly, a survey of college professors in a small, liberal-arts college revealed an inverse relationship between the number of books in a given professor's office and the number of articles he had published in scholarly journals; suggesting that the mere presence of books, while possibly conveying scholarly concerns, can also be explained as an effort to compensate for perceived inadequacies.

Many objects, once vested with certain meanings or culturally ascribed with certain power, can assert a significant influence in our lives, if only symbolically. Objects of religious significance, such as the cross, holy water, eternal flame, or temple signify deep devotion or a divine presence for many. The diamond, the wedding band, anniversary gifts, and flowers have become important symbols of caring in our culture. Some objects, like flowers for a friend and Shakespeare's "sweets to the sweet," have assumed almost universal significance.

Because of the meanings we attribute to them, objects can be valued so highly that they become powerful, controlling forces in our lives. Money has been empowered to signify status, success, and authority; and unfortunately, material wealth also sometimes is seen as a measure of human value. It can become so personally controlling that its loss can lead to tragic and devastating consequences. When equated with human worth, wealth, whether inherited or earned, becomes destructive and disempowering.

Emotions and attitudes as well as social interactions are strongly influenced by perceptions of material objects. The mere presence of a firearm in social situations can increase anxiety and promote aggressive behavior. Conversely, the presence of flowers and plants tends to promote a calm, serene state of mind. The badge, stethoscope, and uniform, all associated with professions, can influence not only our perceptions of the people wearing them, but our emotions and behaviors toward them as well. Our perceptions of objects and the meanings we assign them usually take into account other variables, including the characteristics of the setting in which they are found. Few objects retain a given significance independent of their surroundings.

Of particular interest in our study of psychic empowerment is the "power" or "energy" often attributed to objects as if inherent in the object itself. Although the effects of tangible objects are, for the most part a function of the meanings we assign to them, some objects and certain physical settings do seem to be uniquely energized. Examples are religious shrines with the serenity they evoke; a cemetery that, by its sheer existence, calls forth a somber state of mind; memorials that connect us to those who gave their lives for an important cause; or a special, enchanted place—a secluded beach, meadow, or cove—that inspires faith and renews hope.

The great works of famous artists sometimes have powerful effects on our awareness and appreciation of beauty. This was illustrated by the author, Octave Mirbeau, who, after viewing Monet's series of *Poplars*, reportedly wrote to the impressionist, "In front of the series I experienced an emotion I cannot express, so profound that I wanted to hug you. Never did any artist render anything equal to it."

At another level, even something as mundane as a favorite article of clothing or a piece of jewelry can be endowed with special significance, and even power, that can go beyond the meanings we normally attribute to them. These special objects are often gifts with psychological attachments or associations that signify caring and love. An honor student reported that wearing a birthstone ring given to her by a friend consistently improved her performance on examinations; which she attributed to the ring's psychological significance as well as its special physical features. She believed the stone—an amethyst—generated a frequency of energy that synchronized her own energy system to result in the full activation of her intellectual powers.

In a similar instance, a pre-med student discovered that wearing a certain suit always generated a more positive mental state and brought good fortune into his life. He claimed the suit—a high-school graduation gift from his parents—was consistently empowering, whether worn for examinations, job interviews, or other important events. "Like an old and trusted friend," he insisted, "the suit never let me down." When an emergency illness in his family required his immediate return home, he ceremoniously dressed in his special suit, although he lacked sufficient funds for the trip. "To my amazement," he recalled, "in the vest pocket I found several new bills neatly folded—more than enough money for the trip home. To this day, I cannot explain how they got there." When the suit became too worn for further use, he recycled it by cutting it into patches, which he sewed inside his other clothing. The result, he firmly holds, was a transfer of the suit's original power.

The empowerment potential of objects was strikingly illustrated by the founder of a men's clothing firm who discovered early in his career that a tape measure draped around his neck increased sales. He became so committed to the tape measure that it became a company trademark. He frequently challenged his employees, "If you see me without my tape measure, I will reward you with a new suit." In a similar instance, a famous film director found that his effectiveness on the set was at its peak when he occupied a certain chair. The chair soon assumed the highest respect of the studio and was reserved for the director alone. Other examples of objects that take on special meaning over time are an old but reliable automobile that becomes personalized as a trusted friend, or a homeplace with its treasury of memories, perhaps of childhood.

From the psychic perspective, tangible objects can at times assume a role of life-and-death significance. In a remarkable instance of that role, a simple scrap of paper may have saved the life of a young Wall Street stock broker, who was about to board a subway train. He paused uncharacteristically to pick up a small piece of paper that had drifted by in the breeze and settled at his feet. His pause of only seconds was long enough for him to miss a train that moments later crashed in the tunnel. The insignificant object strangely commanded his attention and possibly saved his life.

SUMMARY

Although we cannot fully explain the complex mental and physical roles of objects as psychic empowerment tools, mastery of strategies employing certain objects could promote psychic growth and effectiveness in applying psychic skills. In the following chapters, we explore the use of several objects in psychic empowerment, with emphasis on possible explanations, effective techniques, and appropriate applications. Although numerous tools and strategies are considered, they share a common goal: the full actualization of our psychic empowerment potential.

CRYSTAL GAZING

~7~

The crystal ball is one of the most widely used tools for stimulating inner psychic processes and expanding psychic awareness. Through the centuries, crystal gazing, or scrying, has been used to probe the unknown; and, in recent years, crystal gazing has been incorporated into a variety of self-empowerment strategies designed to open new vistas of psychic understanding and knowledge. Traditionally, the goal of crystal gazing has been the activation of mental functions specific to various forms of ESP. The technique has proved appropriate, not only in stimulating ESP, but also for achieving other critical self-empowerment goals. Of particular note is its use in arresting and reducing tension, promoting a serene, meditative state of mind, facilitating psychic receptiveness, and heightening the mind's imagery and concentration powers.

The crystal ball is typically situated on a table to promote a downward gaze from a comfortable distance of two or three feet. Mutual crystal gazing can result in significantly higher levels of successful telepathy between individuals or groups. If strategically positioned between sender and receiver, the crystal ball can provide a functional point of focus considered highly conducive to the exchange of psychic information. With even limited practice in crystal gazing, telepathic subjects report dramatic improvements in their capacities to communicate mentally.

Crystal Gazing

In clairvoyance, crystal gazing not only stimulates the essential imagery process, it can activate clairvoyant faculties as well. Clairvoyance frequently appears to originate in the subconscious mind. With practice in crystal gazing, we often can stimulate the inner psychic transfer of important clairvoyant information from subconscious levels to conscious awareness. Furthermore, crystal gazing can become an important vehicle for clairvoyantly connecting conscious awareness to spatially distant unseen realities. For this application, attention is usually focused on the center of the ball, a process facilitated by a crystal ball with a bubble in the center.

For precognition and retrocognition, crystal gazing functions in two important modes: forward and reverse. In its forward mode, the technique transports awareness into the future to reveal selected events, while in its reverse mode, it projects awareness to unknown past events or experiences. For precognition, attention is usually focused on the distant side of the ball; for retrocognition, focus is on the closer side. Both past and future psychic perceptions usually occur as mental images or thought forms, which according to some experienced crystal gazers, are often visible as psychic projections on the crystal ball.

For telepathy, attention is usually focused on the ball's interior regions. Imagery of a channel of light linking the sender and receiver to the crystal ball seems to activate telepathy and increase the accuracy of telepathic communication. The crystal ball, in effect, assumes a functional role as the center of a psychic communication network.

CRYSTAL GAZING STRATEGIES

Because the crystal ball seems to be effective in initiating psychic powers and facilitating psychic processes, a procedure called the Crystal Screen was devised specifically to build the basic skills required to use this tool. The procedure employs a variety of practice articles before introducing the crystal ball itself.

THE CRYSTAL SCREEN PROCEDURE

Step 1   View a colorful picture, giving special attention to the detailed characteristics of color, pattern, and shading.

Step 2 With your eyes closed, generate a detailed mental image of the picture.

Step 3 View a three-dimensional object, such as an article of jewelry or a flower. Focus your full attention on the object's shape and other detail.

Step 4 With your eyes closed, and while holding the object, create a detailed mental image of the object.

Step 5 Replace these practice articles with a crystal ball and focus your full attention on first its surface and then its interior regions. Note specifically such characteristics as reflections, variations in brightness, and impressions of color and depth. Continue the focusing process and allow a tranquil, relaxed state to emerge.

Step 6 With your eyes closed, create a clear mental image of the crystal ball. Take as much time as you need for the image to take shape. Note any physical or emotional effects that may accompany the imagery process. As images continue to form, permit a more relaxed, passive state to emerge.

Step 7 Continue the relaxed, passive state as your psychic receptiveness expands and new images unfold. Concentrate your attention on any image that appears relevant at the moment.

Step 8 Open your eyes and focus again on the crystal ball. Continue crystal gazing, intermittently closing your eyes as you increase your receptiveness to psychic images and impressions.

Crystal gazing also has been successfully applied as a stress management, meditation, and general self-empowerment technique. As a stress management procedure, crystal gazing, accompanied by positive affirmations of self-worth, induces relaxation and a peaceful state of mind. Continued gazing while creating relaxing images such as billowy clouds, a peaceful lake with a sail boat drifting gently in the breeze, or a moon-lit landscape, tends to deepen the empowered, relaxed state.

As a meditation technique, crystal gazing will often produce profound personal insight as well as highly relevant psychic knowledge. A crystal gazing strategy called the "focal shift" generates an empowered mental state conducive to increased psychic awareness and personal insight. Similar to the Peripheral Glow Procedure previously discussed, the four-step strategy which follows usually requires several practice trials to maximize its effectiveness.

THE FOCAL SHIFT STRATEGY

Step 1 Focus your full attention on the crystal ball, then center your attention on a specific area of the ball's surface, such as an area reflecting a point of light.

Step 2 While continuing your focus on a selected area, gradually expand your peripheral vision to take in as much of your surroundings as possible.

Step 3 As your peripheral vision remains expanded to its limits, allow your eyes to shift slightly out of focus. You will notice a whitish glow emerging as your peripheral vision begins to fade.

Step 4 Close your eyes and permit your body to completely relax, as meaningful images and impressions take shape in your mind.

For general self-empowerment, crystal gazing is used to induce a relaxed, empowerment-readiness state as general empowerment affirmations are formulated.

*I am capable and secure; Peace and tranquillity
surround me; I have an abundance of inner
resources; I am empowered to achieve my goals.*

Presented in the context of a generalized empowered state, specific empowering techniques usually are more effective. If your goal is to become a successful architect, for instance, the following general and specific empowerment affirmations may be appropriate:

*I am empowered with success potential. I am surrounded by success. I have all the ability I need to
become a successful architect. I am succeeding in
achieving my goal of becoming an architect.*

These affirmations can be made even more effective through related imagery of an impressive architectural structure that symbolizes future architectural success. Even the most powerful affirmations can be strengthened with related empowering imagery.

The flexibility of crystal gazing as an empowerment strategy is illustrated by its demonstrated effectiveness in a variety of settings. The technique has been used in the academic setting to increase motivation and promote creative thinking. A college instructor reported that crystal gazing, when introduced as an experimental exercise into his course in creative writing, resulted in marked improvements in the quality of ideas and student writing skills. In an experimental industrial situation, an increased number of ideas was noted immediately after the introduction of crystal gazing into a brainstorming session. In competitive sports and the performing arts, crystal gazing has been effective in accelerating the development of skills as well as enhancing competitive performance, when practiced immediately prior to an event.

SUMMARY

Crystal gazing is important in psychic empowerment because of its capacity to engage and liberate the mind's psychic powers. The crystal ball becomes more than an object of beauty; it opens the channels of the mind and permits the free expression of our multiple psychic faculties. The sheer pleasure of crystal gazing, along with the balancing, relaxing, and actualizing effects of the experience, is becoming increasingly recognized as important to personal empowerment. Crystal gazing is pertinent to the quest for empowerment because of its potential to promote not only psychic growth, but also personal well-being.

THE PENDULUM

8

The pendulum—a weight suspended by a chain or string—is an important psychic-empowerment tool primarily because of its capacity to gather highly objective information not available by conventional—or non-psychic—means. In its empowerment applications, the pendulum, suspended from the hand, can be used to answer questions and convey meaningful information by the nature of its motion.

When the pendulum is applied as a psychic tool, the significance of its various movements must be clearly specified. In response to questions posed, a to-and-fro movement is typically designated as a "yes" answer, a side-to-side movement signifies "no," and a circular movement signifies a "cannot say" response. The pendulum can be programmed prior to its application by a simple procedure in which the resting pendulum is instructed, "Give me a 'yes'," followed by a brief interval during which the pendulum's response is noted. Again at rest, the pendulum is instructed, "Give me a 'no'," followed by a brief interval for the pendulum's response.

Advantages to the pendulum as an information-gathering tool emphasize its capacity to respond to very mild energy stimuli. As an extension of the physical body when suspended from one's hand, the pendulum can amplify minute, involuntary muscle activity and thus function as a highly sensitive recording instrument.

The Pendulum

Whether accessing subconscious processes or functioning as an antenna to gather incoming information, the pendulum is a valuable empowerment tool with the potential to explore unseen sources of psychic knowledge.

Many applications of the pendulum emphasize its role in communicating with the innermost part of the self. Within the self is a knowing superintelligence that seeks interaction with the conscious self, but must often rely on indirect means of communication. The pendulum, among other channels, is available to us for engaging that superpower of knowledge.

This perspective of the pendulum's empowerment role does not exclude the capacity of the hand-held pendulum, and other psychic instrumentation, to probe sources of knowledge outside the self. In its clairvoyant application, the pendulum could engage externally charged stimuli to assert a mild but significant influence on either the pendulum or our inner psychic faculties, which then could produce meaningful movement—perhaps psychokinetically—in the pendulum. Such an external influence could explain the usefulness of this tool in applications such as detecting the gender of the unborn. Meaningful movements of the pendulum, when held over the abdomen of the expectant mother, could be explained as a mild gender influence that directly induces motion in the pendulum, or as an indirect phenomenon in which an inner clairvoyant faculty is the mediator. This suggests that subconscious psychic awareness of the unborn's gender could be processed mentally to induce motion in the pendulum. In this way, precognitive content existing in subconscious regions could be transferred indirectly to conscious awareness through the pendulum as an extension of those regions.

The accuracy of the pendulum technique is enhanced through carefully controlled calibration and validation procedures. An excellent validation exercise consists of identifying ESP cards drawn blindly from a deck, by suspending the pendulum over each card, turned face down, while posing questions pertaining to the card's identity. Careful records are maintained of repeated trials to determine the pendulum's level of accuracy. Improvements in accuracy will usually follow repeated trials. Once the pendulum's accuracy level has stabilized, and provided that level is adequate, the pendulum is applied to gather other psychic information.

The pendulum is a valuable psychic tool for gathering information regarding personal concerns. For that purpose, the pendulum is usually suspended over one's own hand or, when applicable, that of another individual, as questions are posed regarding financial investments, relationships, career decisions, and other issues.

In self-hypnosis, the pendulum has both diagnostic and induction applications. When suspended over one's hand, the pendulum can identify barriers or subconscious resistance to hypnosis through questions such as, "Do I really want to be hypnotized?" or "Can I easily be hypnotized?" As a self-hypnotic induction tool, the pendulum is suspended slightly above and in front of the eyes, to facilitate the upward gaze, as suggestions of relaxation and drowsiness are presented. (For this induction approach, an upright, seated position is suggested to prevent injury to the eyes should the pendulum drop as the trance ensues.) This induction approach is more effective if the eyes are permitted to shift slightly out of focus while gazing at the pendulum, thus accelerating the relaxed, drowsy state.

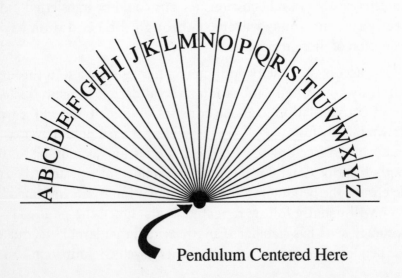

Pendulum Centered Here

The Pendulum Alphabet Chart

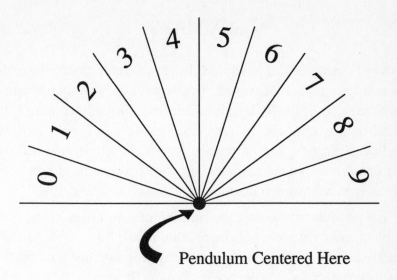

Pendulum Centered Here

The Pendulum Number Chart

As both a precognitive and clairvoyant tool, the pendulum has demonstrated accuracy in gathering information on regional and world events. For this application, the pendulum is held over any relevant object, such as a map for national events or a globe for world affairs. The pendulum can also be used as a dowsing tool for gathering archaeological data or researching historical artifacts, by suspending it over the object being studied.

The pendulum can provide highly specific and complex information when used with alphabet and number charts. Suspended from the hand and appropriately centered over the chart, the pendulum can spell out detailed messages regarding the past, present, and future.

SUMMARY

The popularity of the pendulum in psychic empowerment is due primarily to its demonstrated effectiveness in probing both inner and outer realities. As a simple information-gathering tool, the hand-held pendulum can accurately explore our inner motives, abilities, interests, and potentials. As a probe of external realities, the pendulum can tap distant sources of psychic insight and connect us to a vast wealth of empowering psychic knowledge.

The pendulum is among the simplest of psychic tools, but when applied as an extension of the psychic mind, it becomes part of a highly complex interaction with many empowering possibilities. With even minimal practice, each of us can benefit from the empowering application of this useful tool.

DOWSING

9

An ancient practice that has survived the ages, dowsing has recently been revived as a technique with a host of psychic empowering possibilities. Typically valued as a procedure for locating subterranean resources such as water, precious metals, and oil, the technique usually employs rods of either metal or wood (elm, peach, or witch hazel) as information accessing tools. Over the years, the applications of dowsing have expanded to include modern arenas such as aerospace, ecology, and quality control.

Many accomplished dowsers believe the skill is genetically determined rather than acquired through learning. That claim is supported by the observation of dowsing skills more frequently among blood relatives than in the general population. Controverting that claim, however, are reports among dowsers who say they were trained in the technique by relatives or friends who were accomplished dowsers. The dowsing potential seems to exist to some degree in everyone; and almost everyone, given practice and experience, can become successful at dowsing.

Given a simple rod, or pair of rods, as extensions of the physical body, dowsers have been highly effective in probing the earth's hidden resources and unknown realities. As antennae of the body, and possibly the mind, and when appropriately applied as psychic tools, dowsing rods are believed to stimulate a host of sensory and extrasensory receptors for gathering a vast amount of information.

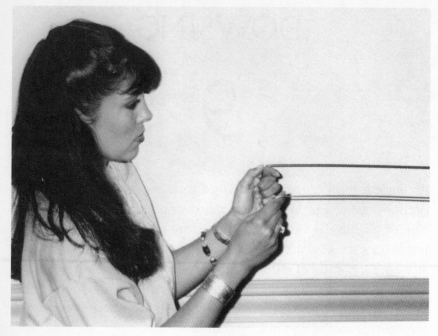

Dowsing

A popular view of dowsing as a psychic phenomenon holds that the rods are extensions of the subconscious mind, and as such, offer indirect, but valuable access to subconscious knowledge. Psychic insight residing deep within subconscious regions could thus become subject to deliberate probes in which the rods function as a spontaneous retrieval device similar to the pendulum.

Because dowsing seems to access inner psychic faculties, it is plausible to assume that dowsing could probe external realities as well: The information derived through dowsing could be viewed as a manifestation or product of clairvoyance. From that viewpoint, dowsing rods are simply external tools of the psychic mind. As the psychic mind develops, so does our capacity for dowsing.

On the other hand, dowsing as a probe of external realities could be explained as primarily a physical phenomenon. The dowser and the rods could act as electrodes and conductors with the capacity to record subterranean activity or other charged environments. If subterranean resources exist with their own unique energy frequencies, dowsing rods, combined with a finely tuned human system, could respond to those frequencies, identifying resources, their locations, and characteristics. This view of dowsing suggests that only a few human systems are sufficiently fine tuned to permit such a delicate interaction. Training in dowsing based on this perspective would emphasize strategies that attune the human system.

When we consider the myriad of potential applications of dowsing, each of these perspectives contributes to our understanding of this complex phenomenon. Rather than a single ability involving a single set of dynamics, dowsing can be explained as multiple abilities involving multiple dynamics which vary from situation to situation. Each dowsing specialty could engage only the abilities specific to that specialty, and the dynamics for each specialty likewise would vary.

Notwithstanding the differences in views and explanations of dowsing, basic dowsing skills can be acquired through even limited guidance and practice. Mastery of the technique's many applications, however, requires practice and the feedback of results along with clearly formulated goals, some degree of motivation, and a recognition of dowsing's empowering possibilities.

As previously noted, dowsing-rod materials vary. For many applications, experienced dowsers prefer L-shaped metal rods designed to be held parallel, one in each hand, with the longer segments of the rods pointing forward. Each rod is balanced along the hand or index finger to permit easy, unobstructed movement.

The rod's typical response movements are the downward-and-upward pull, side-to-side parallel movement, the spreading movement, the crossing movement, and a variety of vibratory signals. Although the interpretation of these responses will vary among dowsers, the downward pull of the rods is typically believed to signal a subterranean resource, with the degree of forcefulness indicating either distance or strength. The experienced dowser usually can gauge both distance and strength based on the nature of the pulling response. A parallel movement, with both rods pulling to the right or left, signifies the location of a strong energy field or natural resource. The separation, or pulling apart, of the rods indicates the border of an energy source located nearby and ahead. The crossing of the rods is usually associated with negative energies that are either repelling to or incompatible with the dowser's own energy system. Radiation, toxic substances, or contaminated conditions will typically induce a crossing movement in the rods. Influences that push the rods apart are usually non-repelling. Examples include water, oil, and most minerals. Vibrations in the rods, whether independent or in conjunction with other movements, typically indicate a powerful energy field.

Some accomplished dowsers prefer twig rods over metal rods. When twig rods are used, they are usually forked. The forked ends are held, one in each hand, with the stem pointing forward. The interpretation of the twig rod's movements is, with a few exceptions, like that of the metal rods: The downward pull signals a subterranean resource, and a left or right movement signifies the position of a resource. An upward pull on the rod indicates a repelling or toxic condition located in either a subterranean or forward position.

The empowering implications of dowsing are extensive. As a technique for gathering information, dowsing has been successfully applied to science and technology, business and industry, forensics, and the military. Valuable subterranean resources including oil, coal, water, minerals, and natural gas have been located through dowsing. In industrial settings, dowsing has been effective in locating buried cables, water, gas lines and valuable resources. In an unusual industrial application, a construction company used dowsing to successfully detect an underground body of water which had been claimed by Native Americans to exist at the construction site. Before excavating, some contractors routinely engage dowsers to determine certain geological characteristics of the site, including water sources, bedrock formations, and the existence of any hazardous conditions.

Skilled dowsers report that the vibratory frequencies recorded by dowsing rods differ for different resources. Frequencies associated with coal are described as tremorous or erratic. Water frequencies are usually described as soft and flowing, and natural gas frequencies are typically described as disruptive to the rods. Radiation, like many contaminants, emits repelling frequencies that cross metal rods and pull upward on twig rods. Unlike other contaminants, radiation also tends to generate impressions of warmth in the rods.

Other uses of this important psychic tool have included: Its application by the military in World War II to locate mine fields, thus saving the lives of many foot soldiers; and its application in locating a treasure of old coins and other gold relics buried on an island off the mainland of Spanish Honduras. In this instance, before on-site dowsing was attempted, a pendulum held over a map of the island identified the general area to be searched. Additional uses of dowsing included its application in locating an abundant subterranean water source which proved more than sufficient in meeting a small town's water demands; and its application by archaelogists to discover valuable pre-Columbian artifacts at an excavation site. Although metal detectors are sometimes used for locating objects such as lost coins, jewelry, and buried metal pipe lines or cables, dowsing is often preferred because of its higher sensitivity and effectiveness in locating metal and specific non-metal materials from a greater distance.

In forensic settings, dowsing has been used successfully to facilitate the investigative effort. In one case, a skilled dowser in a small boat used the technique to locate a weapon that had been tossed into a lake. In another instance, a dowser successfully located a murder victim buried in a shallow grave. Prior to on-site dowsing in each instance, the pendulum was used to identify probable locations by scanning a detailed map of the search area. These applications suggest dowsing could activate psychic faculties such as clairvoyance to expand awareness and reveal important new information. In fact, many dowsers view the technique as primarily ESP, with dowsing rods playing only a supportive or secondary role. However, other dowsers insist that deriving information through dowsing necessitates no psychic functions. They emphasize that skill in dowsing strategies alone is sufficient to access a host of external sources of information.

There is some evidence, albeit controversial, that dowsing may have valuable diagnostic potential when applied to the human body. An example of this application is the use of metal rods to scan the physical body in an effort to identify dysfunctional areas. The procedure usually requires that the subject stand facing the dowser, as the rods, one on each side of the subject, are moved close to the body from the head downward. Any disruption in the frequencies emitted by the body and recorded by the rods signifies an area of stress, organ dysfunction, or damaged tissue. A dysfunction in the cardiovascular system, such as high blood pressure, will emit a continuous, but mild disruptive frequency pattern over the total body; whereas a specific organ dysfunction will produce a localized but intense disruption in the area of the organ involved. This application of dowsing was illustrated by the dowsing scan of a gymnast who had recently sustained a knee injury. Although the injury was unknown to the dowser, the dowsing scan was momentarily arrested when the rods reached the area of the injury. The dowser reported a marked disturbance in the frequencies around the injured knee.

These examples of dowsing suggest exciting possibilities for this extraordinary tool as a useful alternative for probing the unknown and acquiring new and valuable information.

SUMMARY

Dowsing, although an ancient practice, continues to command our interest because of its many contemporary applications and its effectiveness in acquiring important information often unavailable through other techniques. Whether to probe the physical realities of the world around us, to access the inner self, or to engage advanced dimensions of knowledge, dowsing strategies can be readily acquired and effectively applied by almost anyone. Once mastered, dowsing skills enrich our lives with increased awareness, and advance our efforts toward a higher level of psychic empowerment.

THE PYRAMID

☙ 10 ☙

For centuries, the pyramid has been a universal symbol of power and mystery. The Great Pyramid near Cairo is probably the best-known example of this ancient architectural wonder. Built by Pharaoh Khufu (Cheops) during the 2600s B.C., the Great Pyramid is believed by some Egyptologists to have been an astronomical observatory. Others argue that because of the exactness and complexity of its design, it may have represented a meteorological standard. The Great Pyramid provides a permanent record of certain geometric facts: The ratio of the perimeter of its base to its height is almost exactly that of the radius of a circle to its circumference. With the original capstone in place, some theorize that the pyramid may even have served as an energy generator.

The fact that various forms of the pyramid were found in other ancient cultures—in China, Mexico, Italy, Greece, and Assyria—suggests an archetypal significance that could help explain the pyramid's contemporary appeal. Appearing on the reverse side of the Great Seal of the United States is a pyramid with the motto, *annuit coeptis* (He, meaning God, has smiled on our understanding).

Today, the pyramid is often integrated into the architecture of structures ranging from residential dwellings to skyscrapers.

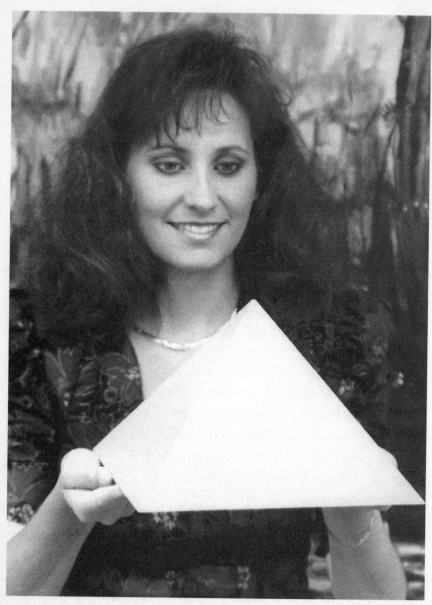

The Pyramid

Adding to the mystery of the pyramid and further reflecting its possible archetypal character, are the contemporary beliefs regarding its empowerment properties. Energizing the self and balancing it with the cosmos are typically cited as examples of the pyramid's empowering capacities. These empowering functions do not seem to be related to either the construction material or the size of the pyramid. A small-scale replica in glass, plastic, wood, metal, or even cardboard seems equally as empowering as the Great Pyramid, provided its orientation and proportional design are exactly those of the Great Pyramid.

The effectiveness of the pyramid as an empowering tool is enhanced to some degree by a personal interest in the object. Although storing the pyramid in a box or displaying it on a shelf as an object of beauty could conceivably be empowering, the deliberate application of the pyramid as an empowerment tool enhances its empowering efficacy, particularly in goal-related situations. Setting personal goals and generating affirmations of success are, of course, empowering independently of any association with the pyramid; but linking goals to the pyramid and incorporating the pyramid into goal strivings can dramatically increase motivation and potential for success. Simply relating the pyramid to our goals gives concrete substance to goal strivings which can be empowering, even in the absence of any intrinsic empowering function of the pyramid.

A popular view of pyramid power centers on the inherent empowering properties of the object itself. This view holds that the pyramid's physical design endows it with certain potential powers, including its inspiring, balancing, preserving, and rejuvenating properties. When the pyramid is oriented with one side accurately aligned to one of the four cardinal points of the compass, its positive potentials are believed to be activated. For most personal applications the pyramid's empowerment potentials are admittedly expanded through appropriate affirmations and a belief in the pyramid's empowering properties.

The physical environment of the pyramid also seems to influence its empowering properties. To induce peaceful, restful sleep and productive dreaming, for example, the pyramid is usually placed under the bed—a placement that can also be effective in enhancing the sex drive. To improve intellectual functions, particularly memory, the pyramid is usually placed in the study area at eye level, if possible. A high-school history teacher noted a remarkable improvement in his students' test performance after he placed a pyramid in a classroom bookcase. In a work setting, the pyramid can be centrally located to promote productivity and harmony among employees, even when they are unaware of the pyramid's presence. Likewise, the pyramid, when strategically located in the home, tends to promote harmony and positive interactions. Some corporations reportedly have pyramids of metal encased in the foundations of their buildings to generate a constructive environment and promote corporate success.

There is evidence to suggest that the pyramid may have healing properties as well. For example, a heart transplant patient, having placed a small cardboard pyramid under his hospital bed, experienced an extraordinarily rapid recovery. He believed the pyramid energized his body and induced a state of balance in his bodily systems, that promoted acceptance of the organ. In a similar instance, a writer with high blood pressure showed a marked decrease in blood pressure after she placed a crystal pyramid on a bookshelf in her study. The sheer presence of the pyramid, she reported, produced a serene, peaceful environment for writing and research.

Many other examples serve to illustrate the pyramid's applications as an empowerment tool. A college student experienced a marked improvement in her test performance after placing a small crystal pyramid under her desk during examinations. A high school physics teacher noted an increase in student motivation and more positive class interactions after she placed a glass pyramid among other geometric objects on her desk. A choral group reported dramatic improvements after a silver pyramid was introduced into the practice and performance sessions. A real estate broker attributed a significant increase in sales to a plastic pyramid positioned under a conference table in his office. A writer noted that a glass pyramid suspended from the ceiling over his computer improved his concentration and stimulated creative thinking. A musician found that holding his hands briefly over a pyramid immediately prior to a concert induced relaxation, enhanced concentration, and improved the quality of his performance. Finally, an experienced gambler attributed his success to a small plastic pyramid he placed at his feet during gambling.

Some of the most dramatic empowering results associated with the pyramid are observed in sports and recreational settings. When the pyramid was introduced into training programs, rapid improvements were noted in activities such as body building, weight lifting, gymnastics, and wrestling. The reported benefits included better concentration, improved motor coordination, and greater endurance.

One of the most valued applications of the pyramid is its apparent usefulness in promoting psychic functions. Some psychics report that the pyramid, when present in their psychic readings, sharpens their psychic skills and generates an environment more conducive to positive psychic interactions. It could be argued that such results are due largely, if not altogether, to the expectancy effects of believing in the pyramid as an empowering tool. Admittedly, recognition and acceptance of an object's empowering potentials, whether real or imagined, would logically increase its empowering effects; but the empowering benefits of the pyramid also are seen in situations where individuals are unaware of its presence. A real estate agency, for instance, reported that the comments of prospective buyers were typically more positive for a building when a pyramid—unknown to the potential buyer—had been strategically placed in the building. A boutique owner reported a sharp increase in sales after she placed a pyramid in a concealed box over the shop's entrance.

PYRAMIDAL STRATEGIES

There is some evidence to suggest that a simple mental image of a pyramid can produce strong empowering results. In the practice of hypnosis, for example, imagery of a pyramid as a post-hypnotic cue has been effective in achieving the goals of reducing stress, losing weight, and breaking habits such as smoking and nail biting. The effects of pyramidal imagery can be intensified through practice in meditation approaches that include empowering affirmations accompanied by images of the pyramid. When used in meditation, pyramidal imagery increases the effectiveness of empowering affirmations and promotes a positive mental state conducive to a variety of empowerment goals. In drug treatment programs, meditative approaches incorporating imagery of the pyramid have been successful in building motivation and the positive self-image considered essential to such programs.

A highly effective meditation strategy called, Ascending the Pyramid, combines imagery of a pyramid and self-affirmations to progressively build a state of peak empowerment. The procedure is initiated by slowing breathing and, with the eyes closed, focusing on the image of a pyramid with ten steps leading to its apex. The ten steps, each with an inscription, are then envisioned one by one, beginning with the first step and culminating at the pyramid's apex, as empowering affirmations are formed. Following are the ten steps with the inscriptions and suggested affirmations for each step:

ASCENDING THE PYRAMID

Step 1 *Love.*

> *Love is basic to my life. It is the energizing foundation of my existence and the center of my being. In my capacity to love, I discover myself and other human beings. Love is the most powerful expression of my being.*

Step 2 *Forgiveness.*

> *In forgiving myself and others, I release the flow of growth potential in my life. Forgiveness is the attitude that characterizes myself and my interactions with others. It is the transforming inner force that soars always upward toward harmony and peace.*

Step 3 *Peace.*

> *Peace is the river that flows through my being. It is deep, abiding, and secure. Infused with inner peace, I can weather any storm that enters my life. Disappointments, misfortune, and uncertainties all yield to the quieting force of inner peace.*

Step 4   *Faith.*

> *Faith is the elevating, activating power in my life. It is my belief in the divine power within my own being. It is the essence of my existence in the universe. In adversity, faith sustains and upholds me. It reveals boundless possibilities in the present and larger dimensions of meaning in the future. Faith is the eternal substance of triumphant living.*

Step 5   *Choice.*

> *Each moment of my life, I am choosing. I choose to think or not to think, to act or not to act, to feel or not to feel. Because I choose, I am responsible for my thoughts, actions, and feelings. They are all mine, and I choose to own them. I am what I choose to be at any moment in time.*

Step 6   *Change.*

> *Change is the current of growth and progress. To become more vibrant, full of life, sincere, and compassionate are changes I value. Positive change carries me always forward to experience something new and vital about myself and the world each day.*

Step 7   *Awareness*.

> *Through expanded awareness, my life is enriched and the meaning of my existence clarified. As I become more aware of my inner self, I become more completely attuned to my being. I know myself best when I come face to face with the totality of my existence in the here and now.*

Step 8   *Knowledge*.

> *Knowledge is power. Through knowing my inner self, I gain power over my life and my destiny. Knowledge empowers me to function more productively and to engage more effectively the future. Given knowledge, whatever its source, I am empowered to bring about needed change in myself and the world.*

Step 9   *Balance*.

> *Balance in my life enables me to be spontaneous and free. My thoughts, feelings, and actions are integrated into a harmonious system that empowers me to adapt to life's demands and to liberate my highest potentials.*

Step 10 *Empowerment*.

> *In my capacity to love, forgive, experience peace, exercise faith, make choices, promote change, expand awareness, discover knowledge, and maintain balance, I am fully empowered each moment of my life.*

The empowering effects of this procedure can be magnified by envisioning oneself pausing at the pyramid's apex and reflecting on the experience. During that reflective state, any of the affirmations can be reaffirmed, and additional affirmations, along with related imagery, can be introduced. The procedure is concluded with the simple affirmation:

I am empowered.

Following practice of this meditation exercise, imagery of the pyramid, independent of the inscriptions and affirmations, can be profoundly empowering. In competitive sports, meditation exercises incorporating imagery of the pyramid immediately prior to an event can dramatically improve the quality of the performance and reduce the number of technical glitches, particularly in activities such as figure skating and gymnastics. In archery, golf, tennis, and bowling, precision was noticeably improved with the introduction of pyramidal meditation, followed by pyramidal imagery at intervals during performance. Similar improvements were seen in sports such as basketball, soccer, and hockey, following team meditation incorporating pyramidal imagery. Performance in any activity requiring precision, coordination, and mental alertness could be improved appreciably through pyramidal meditation and imagery at strategic points during training and competition.

In the academic setting, students who had practiced Ascending the Pyramid, and used imagery of the pyramid immediately prior to course examinations, consistently demonstrated improvements in test performance. Other reported benefits of pyramidal meditation in the academic setting are improved memory of course materials, increased accuracy in problem solving, and greater self-confidence. In courses requiring creativity, students practicing pyramidal meditation reported better instructor ratings of their work.

There is also evidence that pyramidal meditation can be applied to increase the quality of oral presentations. Students in a law program found that practice in pyramidal meditation and imagery resulted in a more relaxed, focused mental state, and greater effectiveness in arguing cases. In one instance, a law student reported rapid progress in overcoming stage fright through simple imagery of a pyramid accompanied by positive self-affirmations immediately prior to a presentation.

Most demonstrated personal empowering benefits associated with the pyramid follow considerable practice of pyramidal meditation strategies, such as Ascending the Pyramid, which are designed to empower through imagery and affirmation. In situations demanding immediate empowerment, just the presence of a pyramid, or a mental image of one, will often work.

SUMMARY

Because of its proven effectiveness in evoking the mind's creative and psychic processes, the pyramid is recognized as a highly useful empowerment tool. Its appeal in the psychic realm is due in part to its capacity to stimulate our psychic faculties by its sheer presence. Its effectiveness in other areas of personal empowerment, however, seems to depend largely on meditation strategies that purposefully utilize this object. When incorporated into empowerment strategies, the pyramid, or images of it, can enrich not only our psychic faculties, but a host of important non-psychic functions as well. The pyramid thus becomes an essential addition to our repertoire of valuable empowerment tools.

TABLE TILTING

⌘II⌘

Table tilting has been practiced widely for many years and continues to be recognized among the psychically empowered as a valuable information-gathering strategy with many potentially empowering benefits. The essential conditions for table tilting are simply a quiet setting and a small group of participants—typically four to six individuals—seated at a small table (usually a card table). After formulating their objectives, the participants typically join hands, reaffirm their goals, and engage in a quiet meditation exercise. They then lightly rest their hands, palms down on the table top, and await spontaneous tilting. The presence of an observing audience seems neither to inhibit nor facilitate the effectiveness of this procedure.

Once tilting has occurred—usually within five to ten minutes—the response is acknowledged as a possible information source, and a communication code is designated: typically one tap of the table on the floor for a "yes" response and two taps for a "no" response, to questions posed either by the participants at the table or by members of the audience. For the duration of the session, the participants' hands continue to rest lightly on the table top. Experienced participants recognize the importance of working *with* the table, not against it. Any intentional effort to physically influence the table's movements can invalidate the results.

Table Tilting

Ostensibly a simple procedure, table tilting is nonetheless a complex and potentially empowering strategy. The technique requires an open, but probing, state of mind, and skill in using the table as a link in a meaningful psychic interaction and communication process. In addition to the basic yes-and-no information provided, an extensive range of table movements can convey highly complex messages. These movements, which we call "table kinesics," include hesitations that usually convey uncertainty, rapid responses that suggest decisiveness, vigorous tappings that can signify either urgency or authority, and slow, gentle tappings that communicate caring and understanding. Occasionally, the table will tap repetitively in response to a single question, an indication that the answer lies in the group, not in the table. At times, the table will pivot precariously on one leg, a response associated with urgency or danger. Only rarely will the table levitate fully, with all legs off the floor; full-table levitation is associated with a profound message or forthcoming revelation. Failure of the table to continue its responses after a series of tappings can indicate either unavailability of information or that the information source is simply no longer present.

The typical table tilting session is concluded with participants joining hands and affirming the potentially empowering benefits of the experience:

> We will individually and collectively benefit
> from this experience. We will use the knowledge
> gained from this experience to promote growth
> in ourselves and others. We are now empowered
> with increased awareness and new knowledge.

Efforts to explain table tilting have centered on two factors: the influence of the group on the table, and the existence of higher planes of energy or other dimensions of reality. We have mentioned that productive table tilting requires receptive participants who are careful not to influence the table's movements. Even in the absence of any conscious intent to influence the table, subtle subconscious motives or the group's combined PK powers could still induce tilting; however, that would not necessarily negate table tilting's empowerment potential. The table could still function as an external channel for the group's subconscious psychic processes, resulting in a manifestation of potentially empowering new knowledge originating from within the group, while at the same time, exercising the group's PK powers.

Another explanation of table tilting asserts the existence of other dimensions of reality—including after-life planes and discarnate sources of insight and knowledge—and says that these dimensions possess the capacity to interact with our reality on the physical plane. From this perspective, table tilting is an empowering interaction between planes, with the potential for a meaningful, rational exchange of critical information.

The discarnate planes perspective of table tilting is based on two assumptions: first, personal existence and conscious being continue beyond death in a state known as discarnate survival; and second, intelligent, deeply personal interactions can occur between physical and spiritual planes, or between incarnate and discarnate dimensions. This would explain the capacity of table tilting not only to engage other planes or dimensions, but also to initiate potentially empowering communication with familiar personalities who have made a successful transition to the "other side."

Table tilting only recently has been recognized for its value as an investigative tool. The technique is especially useful for gathering precognitive and clairvoyant data through the "interdimensional exchange procedure," designed to initiate interactions between physical and non-physical dimensions and energy planes. This procedure is based on a premise that many planes exist, both physical and non-physical, each with the capacity to interact the others. Table tilting evokes this interaction, and thus could enlarge our understanding of the nature of other dimensions and planes, and provide a valuable means of investigating psychic phenomena which appear to involve the merging of other dimensions or planes.

TABLE TILTING PROTOCOL

Following is a complete protocol of a table-tilting session that involved an apparent interdimensional interaction. The participants were college students who had previous instruction in the techniques and theories of table tilting, along with supervised practice in applying the procedure. The session was conducted in a classroom setting, with four volunteer participants seated at a card table, and an audience of thirty students seated in two outer circles. In the protocol, the heading, "Group," identifies statements of participants at the table; the heading, "Audience," identifies statements from the observing students; and the heading, "Table," represents the table's responses. The session began with a brief meditation exercise and statement of objectives by the group. Once tilting occurred, the group designated a communication code related to specific table movements.

Group (*with hands joined*): "We are here to gain insight from the experience of table tilting. We are now surrounded by radiant, protective energy. Our goal is to benefit from this experience by expanding our awareness and increasing our knowledge. We recognize the existence of multiple dimensions and planes as potential sources of important insight and understanding. We are open to interaction with those sources through the table as a communication link. A simple tilting of the table will signify the presence of such a source."

(With hands resting lightly on the table, the group awaited tilting that was preceded by very gentle vibrations in the table. Following a period of approximately five minutes, the table tilted, and while maintaining the tilted position, awaited acknowledgment from the group.)

Group: "We acknowledge your presence and we welcome you to this session. We invite you to interact with us through the table, with one tap of the table on the floor signifying a yes response and two taps signifying a no response to our questions. Will you consent to communicate with us through the table?"

Table: "Yes" (*The table immediately tapped once and upon resuming the tilted position, paused in anticipation of other questions*).

Group: "Thank you. Will you answer questions from participants at the table as well as from the observing audience?"

Table: "Yes."

Group: "Thank you. May we ask questions concerning your identity?"

Table: "Yes" (*hesitantly*).

Group: "Are you from a higher dimension?"

Table: "Yes."

Group: "Have you existed in this dimension we call our physical reality?"

Table: "Yes."

Group: "When did you exist in this physical reality?"

Table: "No response" (*The table had no means of addressing this question since it required a response other than yes or no*).

Group: "Did you exist in this physical reality during this century?"

Table: "Yes" (*immediately and enthusiastically*).

Group: "In that phase of your existence, did you know anyone in this room?"

Table: "No" (*hesitantly*).

Group: "We would like to know more about you. Did you make the transition to the higher dimension when you were young?"

Table: "Yes."

Group: "Were you a child when you made the transition?"

Table: "No."

Group: "A teenager?"

Table: "No."

Group: "In your twenties?"

Table: "Yes."

Group: "Was your death accidental?"

Table: "Yes . . . No" (*The initial one-tap response of the table was followed by a delayed two-tap response, suggesting clarification was needed*).

Group: "Was your death the result of illness?"

Table: "No."

Audience: "Did your death occur in some line of duty?"

Table: "Yes" (*immediately and decisively*).

Group: "Was your death associated with law enforcement?"

Table: "No" (*hesitantly*).

Group: "Was your death associated with the military?"

Table: "Yes" (*instantly*).

Group: "Did your death occur during World War I?"

Table: "No."

Group: "Did it occur during World War II?"

Table: "Yes."

Group: "Did your death occur in Europe?"

Table: "Yes."

Audience: "Did you die in Germany?"

Table: "No."

Group: "Did you die in France?"

Table: "Yes."

Group: "Were you a Frenchman?"

Table: "Yes . . . No" (*This double response indicated a need for further clarification*).

Group: "Were you a French woman?"

Table: "Yes" (*enthusiastically*).

This line of questioning in table tilting illustrates a tendency of many table tilting participants to associate information sources with their own nationality and to assume a personal association with the source. The table tilting source is frequently not only of another nationality but also previously unknown to the group as was the case in this session.

Group: "Were you involved in the French resistance?" (*Some telepathic communication between the source and the table tilting participants may have given rise to this highly specific question*).

Table: "Yes."

Group: "Are you here to share with us what happened?"

Table: "No response" (*Here the table remained tilted, thus suggesting it was time to move to other topics*).

Group: "Will you tell us about your current existence?"

Table: "Yes" (*eagerly*).

Group: "Is that the purpose of your presence here, to share information about the other side?"

Table: "Yes."

Group: "Are you at peace in your current state?"

Table: "Yes."

Group: "Have you retained your identity and past growth?"

Table: "Yes" (*emphatically*).

Audience: "Have you continued to grow since your transition?"

Table: "Yes."

Group: "Is that a part of your purpose for being here, to assure us that our growth will continue after our transition?"

Table: "Yes."

Group: "And that we will retain our personal identity on the other side?"

Table: "Yes."

Group: "In your dimension, do you interact with other personalities who have made the transition?"

Table: "Yes."

Group: "We sometimes call your dimension the other side. Is that an adequate term?"

Table: "Yes . . . No" (*This response seemed to indicate marginal adequacy of the term*).

Group: "Do people from our dimension sometimes visit your dimension?"

Table: "Yes" (*enthusiastically*).

Group: "Through the near-death experience?"

Table: "Yes."

Group: "And through the out-of-body experience?"

Table: "Yes."

Group: "Do we benefit from our interactions with your dimension?"

Table: "Yes."

Group: "Because such interactions prepare us for our own transition into the higher dimension?"

Table: "Yes."

Group: "Do persons sometimes have difficulty making the transition?"

Table: "Yes."

Group: "Because they are overly attached to this dimension?"

Table: "Yes . . . No" (*This double response suggested there were other possible reasons*).

Group: "And because of fear of the unknown?"

Table: "Yes."

Group: "Do we need to be more attuned to the higher dimension?"

Table: "Yes."

Group: "Through experiences such as meditation?"

Table: "Yes."

Group: "And through experiences such as table tilting?"

Table: "Yes."

Group: "Are entities sometimes bound to this dimension in a way that complicates their crossing over to a higher dimension?"

Table: "Yes."

Group: "Are entities ever bound permanently between dimensions?"

Table: "No."

Group: "Are residual energies sometimes left behind by individuals who completed the transition?"

Table: "Yes."

Audience: "Do our two dimensions often interact?"

Table: "Yes" (*enthusiastically*).

Group: "In a way that is mutually beneficial?"

Table: "Yes."

Group: "We have all benefited from this interaction, and we express our appreciation for your presence in this session."

The table gently returned to the floor and the session was concluded with all participants and observers joining hands and affirming:

> *We will use the insight gained through this experience to enrich our lives and the lives of others.*

Almost without exception, table-tilting participants attest to the value of the experience. Frequently, participants report that their lives were profoundly enriched by the experience. Among its many personal benefits and empowering possibilities, table tilting can stimulate our psychic faculties and promote our psychic growth; increase our understanding of ourselves and the nature of our existence in the universe; increase our understanding of the discarnate state; clarify the nature of our spiritual side, affirming the continuation of our conscious identity in the discarnate state; provide highly therapeutic interactions with discarnate dimensions, promoting resolution of grief and offering assurance of survival of bodily death;

promote productive group interactions; serve as an information-gathering tool and research strategy, yielding highly specific evidence of both personal and historical significance; and, finally, enrich our lives in the present and inspire our hopes for the future.

SUMMARY

The emerging contemporary interest in table tilting is partly due to its demonstrated usefulness as an information-accessing tool. Its value as a psychic-empowering tool, for exercising the mind's psychic faculties and stimulating psychic growth and insight, is increasingly being recognized. Given even limited practice, almost anyone can discover its empowering benefits. Furthermore, the technique can be applied almost anywhere. Table tilting reportedly has been practiced in such unlikely settings as corporate board rooms, foreign embassies, seats of government, and even the White House. The future may well see an expansion in the empowerment applications of this useful tool; and the higher faculties of the human mind appear poised to respond.

SAND READING

⮜ 12 ⮞

The tools we have considered thus far—the crystal ball, pyramid, dowsing rods, pendulum, and table tilting—illustrate the effectiveness of tangible objects in facilitating psychic processes. Appropriate application of these objects seems not only to access inner psychic functions and probe hidden realities, but also to activate specific ESP mechanisms and promote overall psychic growth. Each of these objects exists in a stable, concrete form that is unaltered by its use as a psychic tool. Implied in that use, however, is the capacity of the object to directly or indirectly channel psychic knowledge to conscious awareness by initiating some kind of psychic interaction within the mind, or more specifically, between the mind and some superintelligent part of the inner self. When considered from a mystical perspective, the interactions initiated by these tools could also involve some higher plane or supernatural dimension.

Unlike these tools, some objects are effective as psychic instruments only when they have been deliberately acted upon and altered in some way; after which, they can provide a wealth of psychic information. Just as an artist's expressions on canvas can reveal important information about the artist, our expressions in the alteration of objects can reveal important information about ourselves.

This concept provides the basis for a strategy called, "Extrasensory Apperception" (ESA). ESA is a complex phenomenon in which our sensory perceptions of changes produced in external objects are

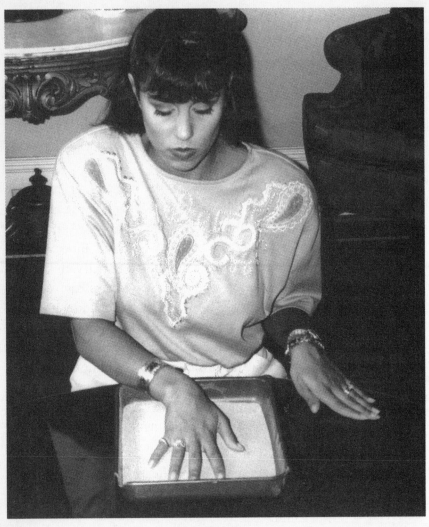

Sand Reading

related to internal psychic elements or faculties, resulting in the stimulation of our psychic processes and the production of new psychic insight. Examples of this strategy are sand reading, a technique practiced in various forms in Egypt for centuries, and the wrinkled sheet technique, a relatively new but highly researched procedure. ESA as a psychic strategy, always requires some alteration of an external, otherwise stable object. Sand reading requires making an imprint of the hand in a tray of sand, and the wrinkled sheet technique requires crumpling a blank sheet of paper into a mass. In both instances, the objects—a tray of sand and a sheet of paper—provide the materials for gathering psychic information only after they are acted upon or influenced in some way.

We all have walked along a beach and noticed footprints in the sand; and we may have speculated about the individuals who had left the footprints behind. In a sense, they had left behind expressions of themselves: Their energies had been captured by the sand to form unique foot-imprint signatures. We may have noted the distinctiveness of each imprint: a record in the sand that could never be exactly duplicated. The imprint might have evoked feelings or impressions about the individual who had left it behind; and, although laden with potential meaning, the imprint was temporary, soon to be erased forever by an ocean wave or breeze.

Like footprints on a beach, a hand imprint formed in a tray of sand is a unique, but temporary expression of the self. When considered psychically, it provides a personal statement that could yield valuable psychic insight. The past, present, and future often merge in a simple hand-imprint signature.

Sand reading requires the subject, whether oneself or another individual, to form an imprint by pressing either hand onto the smooth surface of the sand. Upon removal of the hand from the sand, the remaining imprint provides a valuable information source and essential stimulus for psychic insight to unfold.

In sand reading, objective observations and subjective impressions interact to form the basis for a logical ESA progression.

- *Sensory Perception.* First, the hand imprint and its specific features are objectively observed.

- *Apperception.* Apperception is a conscious, deliberate process in which our objective observations of the hand imprint are associated with subjective, but not necessarily psychic impressions.

- *Extrasensory Apperception.* Our observations of the hand-imprint characteristics and our subjective impressions are associated with inner psychic elements to generate new psychic insight. At this stage, information gathered at various levels of awareness is integrated and psychically processed.

The hand imprint can, on the surface, provide considerable information about the subject that can activate our psychic faculties. For example, we find that the hand imprints of stressed subjects usually have little or no space between the fingers. Although that simple observation alone is important, it can give rise to critical psychic insight regarding the sources of stress, such as marital distress, a career crisis, or a health concern. Even more importantly, psychic impressions concerning solutions and coping strategies will often unfold as sand reading progresses.

Another important attribute of the hand imprint concerns its depth. Men, on the average, tend to press more firmly and to a greater depth in the sand than women; however, unemployed men tend to produce imprints of less depth. Interestingly, unemployment status among women does not appear to influence the depth of the imprint. More aggressive individuals tend to press the hand more firmly into the sand, producing imprints of greater-than-average depth. That pattern was particularly evident in hand imprints obtained from men and women prison inmates who had been convicted of violent crimes. Careful attention to depth can give rise to psychic impressions regarding the sources of destructive aggression, and effective means of coping with emotions such as hostility and frustration, often associated with aggressive behavior.

Very shallow imprints resulting from lightly touching the sand are usually associated with passivity, and may suggest that more assertive behaviors are needed. Some subjects of sand reading will express dissatisfaction with the first hand imprint, and request a second or even third trial. Almost without exception, this pattern seems to indicate either insecurity or compulsive behavior.

Career interests and activities are frequently reflected in the hand imprint. Analysis of the hand imprints of various career groups indicated that imprints in which the thumb digs into the sand are usually characteristic of individuals in skilled or semi-skilled occupations. Imprints in which the little finger shows greater depth are associated with professional careers. It is important to note that imprint-to-occupation correlations are not perfect—there are many exceptions. In sand reading, as with any psychic tool, flexibility and openness to many sources of information and interpretation are essential. ESA recognizes both psychic and non-psychic sources of insight, and the importance of balancing psychic or intuitive impressions with those based on logic and objective observation.

The orientation of the hand imprint in the tray also seems to reflect certain career information. College students preparing for various careers tend to place the hand slightly off-center and to the right of the tray. Retirees tend to orient the hand to the left of the tray. Individuals who are settled into their jobs tend to place the hand in the center of the tray. Interestingly, individuals who are dissatisfied with their careers tend to orient the hand non-perpendicularly, and with fingers pressed together.

Our observations of hand-imprint characteristics of certain vocational groups revealed more variations among the hand imprints of dentists than among plumbers. Dentists also showed, on average, greater depth in the imprints of the little finger, whereas plumbers tended to show greater depth in the thumb imprints. Dentists also showed less space between the fingers in their imprints, a finding that suggested dentists were typically more stressed than plumbers.

Further analysis of the hand imprints of students revealed a strong relationship between imprint characteristics and emotional states. Hand imprints obtained immediately following meditation exercises, such as Ascending the Pyramid, were typically character-ized by a central orientation and considerable space between the fingers. Hand imprints of students under the potentially stressful condition of waiting to take a course examination revealed little or no space between the fingers, and imprints that were almost always non-centrally oriented. In contrast, hand imprints obtained from the same students upon completion of the examination showed greater space between the fingers and a more central hand orienta-tion. Hand imprints obtained under conditions such as watching a TV game show were typically characterized by space between the fingers, but with various orientations. When compared with psy-chological assessment results, hand imprints oriented to the left of the tray were associated with the need to please others and a reluc-tance to assume responsibility, whereas hand imprints oriented to the right of the tray were associated with high achievement needs and independence.

Systematic observations of hand imprints in the clinical setting have suggested possible diagnostic applications of this technique. Anxiety patients, as expected, tend to produce imprints with little or no space between their fingers. Their imprints are typically oriented to the left of the tray, and they frequently express dissatis-faction with the first imprint and request a second trial. Depressed patients tend to use very light pressure in forming their hand imprints, and their imprints are usually non-perpendicularly ori-ented. Analysis of the hand imprints of patients undergoing treatment for substance abuse or substance dependency revealed imprints that were almost invariably placed at the bottom of the tray and oriented to the left.

Sand reading, when introduced into the clinical setting, can be applied as a projection tool similar to the inkblot to provide valuable psychodiagnostic information. In the therapy situation, sand reading can promote a positive therapeutic relationship, while acting as a self-exploration method that promotes self-awareness and insight.

SAND READING AND NUMEROLOGY

Sand reading, as a psychic empowerment strategy, offers a unique opportunity for the introduction of numerology. If, indeed, the world is built on the power of numbers, as claimed by Pythagoras as early as 550 B.C., a number we select at random could have significance for us at any given point in time. That is the basic premise underlying numerology in sand reading. For this application, the subject of the reading, having formed a hand imprint in the sand, arbitrarily selects a number from one through nine, and writes the number anywhere in the sand without overlapping the hand imprint. The number is then interpreted in the light of certain numerologically assigned meanings.

Spontaneity is essential. By selecting the first number that comes to mind, or simply placing the fingertip in the sand and allowing it to automatically form a number, we can ensure the psychic significance and empowerment potential of this exercise. The number selected is considered to be the individual's present, though not necessarily permanent vibratory symbol. It is considered a projection of possible characteristics of the self, as well as a significant representation of the number's possible vibratory meanings. The following assigned numerological meanings are generalizations that are presented as suggested meanings only—there are many exceptions to these suggestions.

The Number 1

This number reflects independence, self-reliance, and a strong achievement drive. As a universal number, it typifies purpose and action. This number is commonly selected by entrepreneurs and competitive sports figures, and people who are strongly committed to a cause.

The Number 2

The vibration of this number signifies antithesis and balance. The subject who selects this number is usually flexible and easy going, while sometimes unpredictable and inconsistent.

The Number 3

This number stands for versatility and talent. Individuals who select this number can usually do many things well, and do not give up easily. They are known to try their hand at many different projects, to frequently change jobs, and to be quite mobile.

The Number 4

Steadiness and solidity are symbolized by this number. People who select the number four are usually practical, trustworthy, and stable. In a crisis, they remain calm, cool, and collected. They are not usually talkative, but when they speak, people tend to listen. Unlike shallow brooks, this number is quiet and deep.

The Number 5

The number five represents adventure. People who write this number in the sand are usually impetuous and romantically involved, often with more than one person. They welcome excitement and even risk. Although their lives tend to be turbulent, they seem to thrive on new projects and relationships, and it is difficult for them to settle down and assume a routine existence. Entertainers, politicians, and actors often select this number.

The Number 6

This is the number of dependability. Individuals selecting this number are typically honest, optimistic, and socially competent; however, they are often stubborn. They have clarified their expectations of themselves, and they tend to impose these expectations on others. They value loyalty in social relationships, and they seek interactions with people who are, like themselves, dependable.

The Number 7

Mystery and knowledge are symbolized by the number seven. It is one of the numbers most frequently selected by psychics and scientists alike. Analytical abilities and complexity are reflected by this number. People who select this number often are intelligent but impractical, independent but vulnerable, and multi-talented but discontented. They are usually conservative, but in social gatherings, they may become the life of the party.

The Number 8

This number stands for success. Individuals selecting this number are usually materialistic and strongly motivated. Although very successful, they are not highly satisfied with themselves; and their dissatisfaction often extends to others, particularly family members. Fathers who select this number are often in conflict with their children, particularly their teenage sons. The number eight man is typically self indulgent, but restrictive with others. The number eight woman is usually forceful, and if married to a number eight man, in competition with him. Her relationships with children in the family are usually better, however, because she uses material rewards to reinforce their achievements, particularly academic success.

The Number 9

Nine is the number of achievement, but achievement as defined here does not necessarily signify material success. Individuals who select this number are interested in global conditions, and they usually express concern for issues such as world hunger and abuse of human rights. This number is often selected by individuals who are actively striving for self-actualization.

Although not included in the range of numbers presented to the subject in sand reading, the number zero will occasionally be selected. This number projects emptiness, loneliness, insecurity, and uncertainty. It is associated with depression, broken relationships, and financial adversity. When asked why they selected the number zero, subjects of sand reading will typically respond, "Because that is the way I feel."

When introduced as an adjunct to sand reading, numerology is a useful empowerment strategy, because it can expand the interpretative possibilities of sand reading and further stimulate self-exploration and empowering new insight.

SUMMARY

A simple surface of sand provides the essential condition for this potentially empowering strategy. Like the potter's clay and the artist's canvas, the sand in sand reading awaits the touch of the hand and the interaction of the exploring mind. The result can be an extensive body of new information and insight. Sand reading offers yet another critical supplement to our repertoire of psychic empowerment strategies.

THE WRINKLED SHEET

ᷞ13ᷞ

Like sand reading, the wrinkled sheet technique is a simple procedure with many empowering possibilities. As ESA strategies, sand
reading and the wrinkled sheet technique can be used together,
because they usually complement each other. Psychic impressions
associated with the hand imprint can often be confirmed or supplemented by patterns appearing in the wrinkled sheet. Frequently,
the hand imprint will reveal aspects of the past and present,
whereas the wrinkled sheet will probe the future.

The wrinkled sheet technique requires a blank sheet of 8½-by-
11-inch paper that is crumpled into a mass by the subject. The
technique can be self-administered to gain information about yourself, or it can be used as a psychic tool to learn about others. When
used for others, the subject is presented with the blank sheet and
typically instructed as follows: "The wrinkled sheet technique is
used as a psychic tool to explore the mind. It requires only a blank
sheet of paper and a willingness to explore. Please write your name
across the top of the page and then crumple it into a mass, just as
you would if you were going to throw it away."

The crumpled sheet is then carefully unfolded and gently
smoothed out with the name side up. The opened sheet is oriented
with the subject's name at the top of the page, ready to provide the
essential raw material for psychic analysis.

The Wrinkled Sheet

The interpretation of the wrinkled sheet begins with the crumpling process itself. A rapid, vigorous crumpling of the sheet, into a relatively small mass, is associated with assertiveness and independence. Men, on average, tend to crumple their sheets more rapidly than women, and their crumpled masses are typically smaller. However, in a study conducted by the author, women executives in a major southeastern corporation took less time to crumple their sheets, and produced masses similar in size to those of their male counterparts. At the top of the executive hierarchy, sex differences in the crumpled masses tended to disappear altogether. These findings suggest the usefulness of the technique, not only to identify the more successful business woman, but also in predicting the probability of success for women in the business world.

A major value of the wrinkled sheet technique is its capacity to stimulate our psychic faculties. Simply holding the crumpled mass in the hands will often activate the mind's psychic functions. The energies expended in producing the mass are recorded in the mass itself, and in a sense, function to hold its crumpled shape in place. Allowing the crumpled sheet to rest lightly in the cupped palm, while opening the mind to emerging psychic impressions, is of particular value in assessing current conditions or identifying pressing problems; but, by unfolding the wrinkled sheet and observing its intricate patterns of wrinkles, we can activate an array of other psychic faculties resulting in the production of totally new psychic insights. Together, the unfolded wrinkled sheet and its counterpart, the unfolded psychic mind provide the essential elements for a potentially empowering psychic interaction.

The application of the wrinkled sheet as a psychic empowerment tool is more effective when it combines both the "whole" and "part" methods of interpretation. The whole method emphasizes general impressions, and looks at overall patterns and the general distribution of wrinkles. The part method focuses on specific elements and targets unique features and small areas of line patterns. Together, these methods provide a comprehensive picture of past experiences, present conditions, and future events.

Attention to patterns—general and specific—and awareness of their potential meanings are essential to interpreting the wrinkled sheet. Once the sheet is unfolded, the variations in patterns are unlimited. No two wrinkled sheets, whether for the same individual or for different people, are ever identical; however, multiple wrinkled sheets produced by one individual do often reveal similar, distinguishable features in their overall distribution of lines, direction of lines, position of clusters, and presence of certain distinct characteristics, such as a well-formed star or circle.

Recurring similarities among patterns for a given individual suggest a stable influence or condition in the life of the subject. A recurring deep line across the sheet can indicate a strong resolve to achieve a particular goal, an unalterable course of events already set in motion, or an early traumatic experience with continuing adverse effects. The psychic mind must determine the relevance of each of these possibilities.

WRINKLED SHEET
PATTERN INTERPRETATION

A number of types of patterns appear frequently in the wrinkled sheet. Following are suggestions for interpretations of some common occurrences.

Straight Lines

Straight lines appearing anywhere in the wrinkled sheet suggest a significant force or influence: the longer the line, the more significant its meaning. Diagonal lines from the lower left to the upper right of the page usually signify progress and future success, whereas diagonal lines from the upper left to the lower right usually signify struggle or a deterring influence. The wrinkled sheets of chemically dependent subjects will often show a strong line reaching from the upper left to the lower right of the sheet. Self-determining and forceful personalities, on the other hand, will frequently produce lines from the lower left to the upper right. A horizontal line can signify stability, determination, personal satisfaction, or conservatism. Vertical lines often indicate risk taking, adventurousness, and restlessness. The wrinkled sheets of compulsive gamblers nearly always will show several vertical lines.

Clusters of Wrinkles

Clusters are produced by many intermeshing small wrinkles. Clusters can represent a complex such as inferiority, a talent that is musical or artistic, a turbulent mental state such as depression, or an entangled relationship. The psychic mind must sort through these and other possibilities to find the true significance of the pattern.

The *location* of the cluster can provide a clue to its meaning (See Quadrant Map and Interpretative Guide for Clusters in the Wrinkled Sheet). A cluster in the center of the sheet typically signifies a prominent concern. A series of wrinkled sheets for a young male executive consistently revealed a cluster in the center of the sheet. When it was pointed out that this pattern often signaled a current dilemma, he confided that his troubled marriage was threatened by divorce.

Clusters oriented toward the left side of the wrinkled sheet are typically associated with past influences and early experiences. When situated toward the right, clusters can reveal a significant future development. An attorney running for public office consistently produced a cluster in the lower right quadrant of the wrinkled sheet, suggesting highly tenuous circumstances. Although he vigorously continued his campaign, he was severely defeated. Conversely, a secretary planning a business venture produced a strong cluster in the upper right quadrant of her wrinkled sheet, a position favoring future success. She proceeded with her plans and successfully established a highly profitable business.

The quadrant location of a cluster in the wrinkled sheet reveals both time and intensity clues: The closer the cluster to the central vertical line, the closer to the present; and the higher the cluster on the page, the more positive the influence.

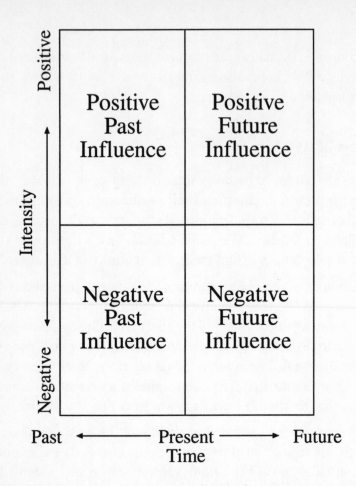

Quadrant Map and Interpretative Guide for Clusters in the Wrinkled Sheet

Crossed Lines

Two perpendicular lines that cross are associated with strivings, conflict, and ambivalence. As with clusters, the position of the crossed lines provides critical time and intensity clues (See Quadrant Map and Interpretative Guide for Crossed Lines in the Wrinkled Sheet). Crossed lines appearing on the left side of the page suggest unresolved past conflict; while crossed lines on the right side of the page predict future discord. Crossed lines at the center of the sheet reflect current strivings. A college student experiencing ambivalence

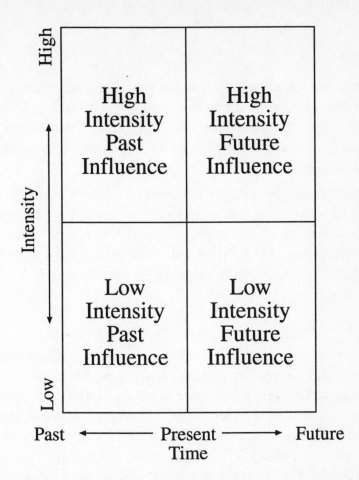

Quadrant Map and Interpretative Guide for Crossed Lines in the Wrinkled Sheet

regarding his future career consistently produced crossed lines in the central area of his wrinkled sheet. Highly anxious individuals will often produce wrinkled sheets with prominent crossed lines in the upper quadrants of the page. Crossed lines in the lower quadrants typically signify conditions of lesser intensity.

The location of the crossed lines reveals both time and intensity clues: the closer the crossed lines to the central vertical line, the closer to the present; and the higher the crossed lines on the page, the more intense the influence.

Triangles

A triangle, appearing anywhere in the wrinkled sheet, is associated with a three-dimensional problem situation, with each side of the triangle representing one facet of the problem. These are usually asymmetrical, with the longer side of the triangle representing the dominant element or influence in the problem.

Romantic triangles are often indicated by triangles. A college student, torn between his fiancee and a new love interest, produced a wrinkled sheet with a prominent, asymmetrical triangle at the center. He interpreted the longer side of the triangle to represent himself and his vacillation in the triangle situation.

Circles

Good fortune is symbolized by circles appearing in the wrinkled sheet. Circles can predict career advancement, business success, and financial prosperity. Just prior to his appointment to a prestigious political post, a government official produced a wrinkled sheet with a large, near-perfect circle near the center of the sheet. Immediately before a job interview, a doctoral student's wrinkled sheet revealed a circle in the upper right quadrant of the page. He was soon notified that he was a successful candidate for a highly competitive position. Although the absence of a circle does not necessarily indicate misfortune, the presence of a circle is always considered a good omen.

Squares

Squares are usually considered foreboding when they occur anywhere in the wrinkled sheet. On the left side of the page, a square unusually indicates negative influences that have already been activated, and in the absence of intervention, could culminate in adversity such as entrapment, betrayal, financial loss, or other misfortune. An investor's wrinkled sheet, just prior to a significant financial loss, revealed a clearly formed square of unusual symmetry near the center of the page. In a more tragic vein, a wealthy industrialist, whose daughter was later abducted, produced a wrinkled sheet with two large squares, one near the center and the other in the lower right quadrant of the page. Typically, larger squares reflect more serious misfortune.

Hearts

Only rarely will a heart appear in the wrinkled sheet. Invariably, a heart symbolizes romance, although when it appears near the bottom of the page, it signifies a less than satisfying love relationship.

Stars

A star appears as a symbol of psychic giftedness. A well-known psychic from London produced a wrinkled sheet with four, perfectly formed stars—one in each of the sheet's quadrants. A four-pointed star indicates rich, but underdeveloped psychic potential, whereas a five-pointed star is associated with highly actualized psychic abilities.

Pyramids

The pyramid is the rarest of all patterns observed in the wrinkled sheet. It is usually formed by three or more triangles merging to produce a raised form. Even when the sheet has been smoothed out, the pyramid will retain its slight elevation. Like the star, the pyramid is a symbol of psychic giftedness. When it appears with a star, the pyramid signals extraordinary psychic power. The inverted pyramid, however, suggests a loss or deterioration of psychic power, or a denial of one's psychic potential.

Abundant Wrinkles and Clusters

Usually observed in the wrinkled sheets of highly active individuals whose interests are varied, and who are engaged in many activities, this pattern can indicate disorganization, impulsiveness, and scattered energies.

Parallel Lines

A pair of lines that are parallel to each other is associated with social interests and personal relationships. A high frequency of parallel lines suggests strong social interests. The isolated occurrence of a pair of lines symbolizes a specific personal relationship. The strength of a relationship can be gauged by the closeness of the two lines, with lines closer together signifying a stronger or more intimate relationship. The duration of the relationship can be gauged by the length of the lines: parallel lines that fade or separate toward the right side of the sheet suggest a future weakening of a relationship. When they appear near the top of the wrinkled sheet, parallel lines usually indicate relationships that involve strong commitment or emotional investment. Parallel lines appearing in the lower half of the sheet suggest a more physical relationship, or a relationship based on practical considerations.

Intricate Patterns

Highly intricate patterns, that include many complex clusters generously distributed throughout the sheet, are associated with complicated life situations. Less intricate patterns and fewer clusters suggest a simpler life style. Individuals whose lives are highly structured and controlled will often produce a wrinkled sheet with very few intricate patterns.

Strong Creases

Wrinkles that form strong, and sometimes raised creases are associated with assertiveness and independence. The wrinkled sheets of high-achieving men and women typically reveal strong creases.

Tears

Occasionally a tear will appear in the wrinkled sheet. When it occurs at the sheet's edge, a tear suggests a tendency to act on impulse, and to rely on feelings rather than facts when making decisions. When the tear occurs elsewhere in the sheet, it reflects a potential crisis or traumatic event.

Although careful attention to detail is essential in interpreting the wrinkled sheet, more general or global impressions of the overall pattern can give rise to important psychic insight. When the apperception process is appropriately activated, each external observation will trigger a function of the psychic mind to aid in interpretation.

It is important to emphasize that any given characteristic in the wrinkled sheet can have many potential meanings, and these can vary widely. A single pattern can signify a journey for one individual, a lifestyle for another, and goal-striving for yet another. A pattern of lines oriented diagonally from the lower left to the upper right can suggest financial success for one subject and self-fulfillment for another. A cluster of wrinkles can mean emotional upheaval for one individual and an organized plan of action for another. The answer lies in the psychic mind, and only when processed by the psychic mind can the wrinkled sheet fulfill its potential as an empowerment tool.

SUMMARY

The avenues for exploring the mind, like the mind itself, are endless. The wrinkled sheet technique, like sand reading, provides in symbolic form, a representation of the innermost self. Its intricate complexity parallels the complexity of the human psyche, and when appropriately interpreted, provides yet another valuable source of psychic insight. In our continuing struggle for wisdom and understanding, the wrinkled sheet can offer the critical raw material for activating the creative, inquiring mind. The exquisitely complex wrinkled sheet effectively engages its counterpart, the exquisitely complex mind; the greater our psychic skills, the more easily we can make that subjective leap into psychic space.

AUTOMATIC WRITING

～14～

As a psychic empowerment strategy, automatic writing is based on two important concepts: first, information existing in the subconscious regions of the mind persistently seeks manifestation in conscious awareness; and second, indirect channels, including automatic writing can activate inner psychic faculties and access hidden sources of knowledge when more direct channels are either unavailable, or if available, are less efficient.

Automatic writing is a psychic accessing strategy in which spontaneous or involuntary writing is used to bring forth information from the subconscious mind. The technique is believed by some to tap into other sources of knowledge as well, including higher planes. Usually, the only materials required are a writing pen and paper. The pen is held in the writing position with the point resting lightly on the writing surface, as meaningful written messages are permitted to unfold.

A brief relaxation and mental-clearing exercise, in which physical tension is released and active thought is minimized or banished altogether can increase the effectiveness of automatic writing.

The initial products in automatic writing are often illegible; but once meaningful writing emerges, the technique can provide important messages about the past, present, and future. Automatic writing can consist of a single, but significant word, sentence, or phrase; and occasionally the technique will produce a drawing or other meaningful symbol. Although the technique often is used in an open-ended fashion, as a completely spontaneous expression of the self, it can be used to gather answers to specific questions or to find solutions to particular problems. At advanced levels, it can access highly significant sources of psychic knowledge. For instance, a woman who had been given up for adoption at birth, used automatic writing to successfully locate her biological brother. In another case, a writer used automatic writing to create the names for characters in a short story. Still other examples include a college student who used automatic writing to develop major ideas for a research project; an industrial firm which engaged a psychic consultant to explore the company's expansion options; the consultant who identified an option which, once implemented, resulted in a highly successful new product line; and a psychic consultant who used automatic writing to gather critical information that led to the solution of a series of crimes.

Because of its capacity to tap into the psychic mind and channel messages, automatic writing, as a psychic accessing tool, has almost unlimited psychic applications. Precognitively, the technique can tap into the future and provide information needed for planning and decision making. At the advanced level of this technique's clairvoyant and precognitive applications, no reality can escape the penetrating probe of the psychic pen.

As already noted, automatic writing, as a psychic empowerment procedure, is more effective when preceded by a brief period of meditation, during which affirmations are presented which are designed to prepare oneself for the exercise and to program the technique to explore the psychic sources of knowledge.

My psychic mind is now responsive to the probes
of automatic writing. The information I need will
become available to me through this empowering

technique. Through automatic writing I can acti-vate my inner psychic faculties to endow me with insight and expanded awareness. The one hundred billion cells of my brain await the empowering intervention of automatic writing. Through automatic writing, the deepest recesses of my mind will yield their empowering secrets.

These general empowering affirmations are usually followed by specific queries designed to address an unlimited range of concerns.

How can I increase my psychic powers? What investments should I consider at this time? What do I need to know about my future? In what career field will I find greatest satisfaction?

When automatic writing is used to discover a specific answer, the question is usually written at the top of the page before beginning the process.

The effectiveness of automatic writing as a psychic tool is directly related to the spontaneity of the process. Any conscious intent to influence the process can negate its psychic significance. With conscious functions subdued and the physical body sufficiently relaxed, our psychic channels can be activated, and the sources of psychic insight accessed, through this empowering technique.

Through automatic writing, past experiences lost to conscious awareness are often brought forth. This phenomenon was illustrated by an armed robbery witness who used automatic writing to retrieve crucial information about the crime. Through the highly specific information produced by automatic writing, including a thorough description of the perpetrators and the get-away vehicle, investigators were successful in promptly solving the case.

One of the most important empowering applications of automatic writing is its therapeutic role in probing the subconscious for strivings, motives, and conflicts buried within the self. Knowledge and insight can be brought forth as a new surge of personal awareness and power. Note that the subconscious mind typically yields only the information we are prepared to accommodate at the time: A chemist who experienced frequent anxiety attacks used automatic writing to discover the hidden sources of her distress. A victim of sexual abuse in childhood, she had buried the painful experience in her subconscious mind. Unfortunately, repressed experiences, though outside conscious awareness, continue to assert their disempowering effects typically in the form of either painful anxiety or some exaggerated defense mechanism. Upon finally discovering the source of her anxiety through a series of automatic writings, the chemist was able to resolve the conflicts surrounding the abuse, and successfully overcome the anxiety that had plagued her for many years. This example of automatic writing reflects the advanced therapeutic skills of the subconscious mind. Through automatic writing, the therapeutic mind spontaneously yielded critical, but painful information, while at the same time providing the coping resources essential to her recovery. Indeed, the model therapist exists within each of us. Automatic writing is but one of the many strategies that can connect us to that healing part of the inner self.

A major advantage of automatic writing over other psychic accessing strategies concerns the *nature* of the information the procedure can produce. The information yielded by some psychic tools is highly constricted, and in some instances limited to simple "yes" or "no" responses. Automatic writing, on the other hand, can address such concerns as what, when, where, why, and how. At its most advanced level, automatic writing is limited only by our willingness to yield to our subconscious faculties, and by our capacity of written language to communicate. Achieving that optimal level requires skill in consciously surrendering to the inner, knowing part of the self and allowing its written expression.

Because it is not subject to the screening and suppressive functions of consciousness, automatic writing, once mastered, offers a direct line to the vast powers of the subconscious mind. The superintelligent part of our inner self is accessed and liberated, resulting in a full and free expression of our inner powers.

Automatic writing can overcome the language barriers that often thwart inner communication. Among its major functions is the translation of subconscious images into a meaningful conscious reality: the written word. Imagery is the native language of the subconscious mind, and as such, it is the most powerful language known. Imagery can convey an almost unlimited range of emotions and knowledge. Incipient imagery has been the embryo of major scientific inventions, new discoveries, and even global change. Seminal imagery can provide us with a challenging vision of our highest destiny, and empower us to achieve our loftiest goals. Through imagery we can get a glimpse of the vast regions of our inner world of awareness and stored experience. Automatic writing can tap into that inner powerhouse to permit direct, undisguised written expressions of empowering insight.

Automatic writing can enrich our psychic faculties and expand our capacity to actively communicate and interact with the inner self. Inner psychic communication channels—dreams, intuitions, and psychic impressions—can be supplemented and clarified. Many psychic communications occur in disguised or symbolic forms that require a concentrated effort to glean the essential substance of the message. Automatic writing is a powerful tool for disrobing the disguised figure of psychic communication. An impression of a rose can symbolize a developing romantic relationship; whereas a psychic impression of a whirlpool can represent a social relationship spinning out of control and overwhelming us. Automatic writing can be applied to glean the true meaning of these symbols from among the many possibilities.

Psychic messages, including many of our dream messages, can occur in antithetical form: an impression of death can signify birth, and an impression of joy can signify sadness. Fortunately, the antithetical impression is usually accompanied by a clue that reveals its antithetical nature, such as an additional, but incongruent impression. Aside from antithesis, many psychic impressions are so general that deciphering their specific meanings can be very difficult. Automatic writing can be a useful tool for exploring the antithetical possibilities and true meanings of these disguised psychic signals. For this application of automatic writing, the sentence completion technique has been highly effective. Some examples of unfinished sentences are:

"My impression of danger means...";

"I need to concentrate on...";

"I will find happiness in...";

"My life is...";

"I can profit from...";

"I predict...";

"It is important that..."; and,

"My future...."

Automatic writing, as an adjunct to dream analysis, can follow each dream element to its root, and unleash empowering nutrients to permeate the self with new vigor and growth. A word-association method can help decipher the dream's symbolic meaning, using automatic writing to amplify and expound on the written dream symbol. Following are selected examples of dream symbols and their meanings as derived through automatic writing:

Dream Symbol	Meaning
Bridge	Change and opportunity
Earthquake	Loss of valued possession
Falling	Out of control
Fire	Anger that can be destructive
Fog	Go slowly, but don't give up
Letter	Listen to your inner self
Moon	Future romance
Ocean	Destiny
Sunrise	A new beginning

An expanded list of dream symbols and their meanings is found in the Appendix of Dream Symbols at the end of this book. Because a given dream symbol can have many interpretations, automatic writing is a useful tool for sorting through those possibilities and identifying those most relevant. The effectiveness of automatic writing in dream analysis requires practice and a willingness to explore the secret recesses of the mind. We are the best interpreters of our own dreams, and within each of us is an expert dream analyst who awaits our purposeful probes. Automatic writing equips us to engage that inner analyst in an empowerment interaction that can unleash an abundance of new insight and growth possibilities.

SUMMARY

Aside from its complementary role in facilitating psychic processes, automatic writing can function independently of other psychic channels. It can directly probe the future, activate repressed faculties, initiate empowering dialogue, and generate new psychic knowledge and understanding. In its ultimate form, automatic writing can connect us to the central core of our existence; it can channel universal wisdom and manifest it materially as a visual, written message.

Any skill that unleashes our capacity for self-expression and discovery is essentially self-empowering. Automatic writing is valued as a psychic empowerment tool because it achieves that important goal.

THE OUT-OF-BODY EXPERIENCE

ᔐ 15 ᔑ

Reports of the out-of-body experience (OBE) commonly describe the phenomenon as "enlightening," "profound," "spectacular," and "empowering." Out-of-body experiences—also called "astral projections" or "astral travels"—are states of awareness encompassing a conscious sense of being in a spatial location away from the physical body. The out-of-body concept assumes a duality of human nature, and the existence of an extrabiological consciousness or astral double. OBEs further assume the capacity of the extrabiological to disengage the physical body, and in that disengaged or out-of-body state, to travel consciously to experience distant realities.

OBEs can occur both in the normal state of awareness and in altered states such as sleep, hypnosis, and meditation. The out-of-body state itself could be considered an altered state. However, it is distinctly unlike other states of consciousness in that it is usually accompanied by a profound awareness of separateness from the physical body. Although OBEs are sometimes described as dream-like in nature, they appear to be expressions of the disengaged extrabiological state rather than simply the products of sleep. Furthermore, the OBE subject often chooses a destination and brings back clear, conscious recall of the experience. It is conceivable that what sometimes appear to be lucid dreams are, in reality OBEs.

In recent years the out-of-body experience has become the subject of increased interest and speculation, not only because of the numerous reports of the phenomenon, but also because of an emerging recognition of its potentially empowering value. Although some claim that OBEs exist only in the mind, others firmly hold that these are valid phenomena with many empowering possibilities.

One view of OBEs considers the sleep experience itself to be an out-of-body state in that, as we sleep, the non-physical or extrabiological double is thought to hover over the physical body. The experience of falling asleep could involve literally a "falling out of the body" or a drifting away of the astral from the physical body. Supportive of that perspective is the fact that drifting into sleep is often accompanied by sensations of being borne aloft, or of flowing away from the physical body. Any sudden disruption of that drifting astral experience seems to result in an unpleasant or jolting re-entry. This view further holds that sleep, as an out-of-body state of projected consciousness, is highly conducive to out-of-body travel; but out-of-body travel is thought to occur only when the projected astral body moves to a spatially distant location to experience other realities. The typical dream experience, which often includes symbolism and distortion, is more likely an expression of the subconscious. On the other hand, dreams of drifting over terrain and vividly experiencing other realities that are free of distortion could, arguably at least, be explained as astral travel, rather than subconscious manifestations or other dream products.

We encounter situations daily that could spontaneously evoke the out-of-body experience. Many OBEs are thought to occur in unrecognized form, or at least, are not consciously labeled as out-of-body. Examples are losing track of time or any unaccountable loss of a block of time, being lost in thought or caught up in fantasy, and a variety of reflective, musing states.

Notwithstanding the many reports and mounting evidence supporting OBEs, conventional science remains reluctant to accept the existing data. This is in part due to the elusive and subjective nature of the experience and the often inconclusive results of OBE research. These problems, along with the admittedly biased views of many researchers, have constricted research efforts and in some instances, shrouded the topic with undue mystery. Not surprisingly then, many individuals who experience the phenomenon reject it outright, or they anxiously question its normality.

For many people, however, the out-of-body experience is profoundly meaningful. A psychologist recalled an out-of-body experience that may have literally saved her life. Prior to a serious automobile accident, she experienced troubling, recurring dreams in which her car overturned several times. When the accident finally occurred, she spontaneously entered the out-of-body state, during which she watched her car from above as it overturned several times down an embankment, exactly as seen in her dreams. She walked away from the accident without injury, and attributed her escape to the out-of-body experience which gave her physical protection at a time of great danger.

Typically absent in the out-of-body state are experiences of pain and distress or physical and mental limitations. Furthermore, OBEs, as empowering phenomena, have reportedly accelerated recovery from certain physical and mental impairments. Of particular interest are reports that impairments associated with damage to the central nervous system are absent in the astral body during OBEs. This was illustrated by an athlete, partially paralyzed by a spinal injury, who reported frequent OBEs during which he functioned normally and experienced no discomfort. He attributed his remarkable recovery to OBEs that enabled him to exercise his body mentally while stimulating the damaged regions of his nervous system. In a similar instance, a stroke patient confined to a wheelchair, reported OBEs in which the astral body functioned normally. She attributed her recovery to the mental exercise provided by her recurring OBEs. She saw the OBEs as stimulating healing and literally repairing the specific brain areas damaged by the stroke. In another instance, a policeman, partially paralyzed by an injury sustained in the line of duty, reported daily OBEs in which he experienced no impairment of astral body functions. He valued the out-of-body experiences for their enrichment and motivational benefits, as well as their actual physical effects in accelerating his eventual recovery. The physical benefits of OBEs are further illustrated by the reports of a young executive who suffered from tinnitus, a persistent and distressing ringing in the ears that often impaired his ability to concentrate. He discovered that upon entering the induced, out-of-body state, the ringing in his ears abruptly ceased. Upon his return to the body the ringing resumed, but with less intensity. He began practicing OBEs daily as a means of relieving the ringing. Eventually, the ringing that had plagued him for years permanently ceased.

Although spontaneous OBEs are associated with normal, every-day activities, they can occur under conditions that are intensely stressful. For instance, a prisoner of war, while being interrogated by his captors and subjected to excruciating pain, experienced the spontaneous sensation of drifting away from his physical body. Free from pain in that projected state, he saw his physical body lying apparently lifeless on the floor. He recalled the out-of-body experience as profoundly empowering, because it enabled him to cope with otherwise intolerable pain, and perhaps even more importantly, it strengthened his will to live. He attributed his survival and eventual escape to the empowering effects of the out-of-body experience.

There exists some evidence to suggest the possibility of PK during the out-of-body state. The capacity of the mind in the out-of-body state to influence external events seems to be enhanced in dangerous accident or near-accident situations, typically for the purpose of preventing injury. This concept, which we call, "out-of-body PK," was illustrated by an equestrienne who, upon being thrown from her horse, immediately entered the out-of-body state, and while viewing her fall from a distance, slowed the fall and cushioned the impact, thereby escaping the fall uninjured. In a somewhat similar instance, a student spontaneously entered the out-of-body state upon losing his balance when stepping from his shower. While viewing his fall from overhead, he mentally directed his body away from the dangerous edge of the tiled shower opening, thus preventing a possibly serious injury. These instances of spontaneous out-of-body PK reflect the mind's psychic vigilance, and its remarkable capacity for immediate, powerful intervention when needed.

OBEs are often valued as a source of personal pleasure, as illustrated by a writer and her husband whose careers required frequent travel and lengthy separations. Both were skilled at out-of-body travel, so they decided to use OBEs as a vehicle for intimacy. They designated certain times and places for their out-of-body rendezvous during periods of separation. They insisted that these out-of-body intimacies were highly gratifying, both emotionally and physically. For this application of OBEs, they noted that "my place or yours" could be anywhere in the universe, from the exotic Orient to the enchanted Caribbean, or even some distant planet among the stars.

Among other reported applications of the out-of-body experience is its usefulness as a search strategy for locating lost objects and missing persons. In one celebrated case, a psychic's out-of-body search accurately located a plane crash in a remote mountainous region. Similarly, a parcel of narcotics known to have been dropped somewhere on an island was located through a consulting psychic's out-of-body search. Even lost animals have been located through this search strategy. A physician whose cat had strayed, reported a spontaneous out-of-body experience during sleep in which she successfully located the lost animal. Scanning the neighborhood from above, she saw the cat sitting on the steps of a vacant building several blocks from her residence. She awakened in the night, drove to the abandoned building, and found the cat on the steps exactly as seen in her out-of-body search.

OBEs are often viewed as expressions of our spiritual side. Possibly one of the most profound implications of OBEs concerns survival of bodily death and the permanence of our conscious being. If personal identity remains intact in the state of temporary astral disengagement from the physical body, it could be argued that following bodily death and the resultant permanent disengagement from the physical body, non-biological consciousness and identity would likewise survive. Supporting that argument are numerous accounts of near-death experiences (NDEs) during which meaningful out-of-body interactions with other dimensions occurred. Many of these accounts detail active participation in distant realities and significant interactions with others who had successfully completed the transition to the other side. NDEs can be so profoundly meaningful that perceptions of life and death are permanently altered by the experience. That phenomenon was illustrated by a clinical psychologist who reported a near-death experience following a cardiac arrest, during which he was guided by an angelic presence to a place of indescribable beauty. He recalled entering a garden and recognizing his deceased mother waving happily to him from a distance. He was then gently guided back to his physical body. The experience was so intensely meaningful that the psychologist's beliefs about life and death were deeply affected.

OBEs, like other forms of psychic phenomena, are inherently empowering, because they expand our capacities to experience realities beyond the scope of biological mechanisms alone. Some of these realities, like the superintelligent part of our being, are within ourselves, and some exist as distant physical environments. Others appear to exist as higher planes, or as dimensions quite unlike the familiar realities we have come to know through the channels of our physical senses. Possibly our most valuable empowerment faculty is our capacity to transcend the physical world and experience realities of a higher, spiritual plane. Many OBEs and more specifically NDEs clearly reflect that empowering, transcending part of our being. Subsequent to the near-death event, death is often seen not as an end of existence and awareness, but as a transition to a higher plane of enriched experience. For many who encounter near-death, life after death is clearly confirmed not as some meaningless state of nothingness, but as continued, conscious, purposeful, and exciting existence.

Basic to human nature is the need to experience meaning beyond that possible through sensory perception and biological experience. Philosophers and theologians address that human search for significance; but resolving the issues and discovering the meanings of life demand personal investment and self-involvement. Only when we are committed to probe the mysteries of our being can we know the deeper meanings of life and death, reality and experience, and finally, the full scope of existence itself. Because it disengages the biological body and frees consciousness to soar, the out-of-body state provides a valuable vehicle for exploring the unknown and discovering hidden realities. OBEs often reveal the missing conceptual link between ultimate concerns such as mortality and immortality, existence and non-existence, being and non-being, and the physical and the spiritual. OBEs are often so penetrating that they give clear substance to our hopes for permanence and firm confidence in our spiritual destiny.

As noted previously, OBEs are different from other forms of psychic phenomena because they require a separation of two human systems: the biological and the astral or extrabiological. This concept, which we call, the "two-component disengagement principle," views the extrabiological as the embodiment of consciousness, or the soul of being, with the capacities to think, perceive, learn, feel, and grow. As an indestructible entity, the extrabiological becomes our energizing life force, the essential element and core of existence itself. It is not surprising that the meaning of OBEs is often greater than experience that is limited to sensory stimulation and perception. The out-of-body state effectively subdues the biological inhibitors of experience and sheds biological baggage to permit conscious awareness to flow freely.

The two-component disengagement principle holds that the physical body is the instrument of the psychic mind. As such, our physical system is endowed with certain empowering capacities—sensory, autonomic, defense, and regulatory systems—that facilitate our functioning in the world. The seat of our human powers, both physical and mental, is not the body, but the mind. Our limited physical capacities are transcended by the unlimited powers of our inner being. The two-component disengagement view explains why human experience continues in uninhibited and even enriched form in the out-of-body state.

Transcending experiences during OBEs often do not translate well to mundane consciousness, since neither our biological systems nor our language reference is sufficiently equipped to permit such a translation.

Exceedingly complex mental processes and a wide range of rich emotions characterize many OBEs. Furthermore, sensory-like functions such as sight, hearing, taste, and smell continue in the out-of-body state. A host of pleasurable emotions including joy, contentment, peace, and serenity typically occur; while experiences of sadness, fear, anxiety, and distress are absent. Individuals who are inexperienced in out-of-body travel will occasionally report some apprehension upon first entering the induced out-of-body state; but with even limited practice, almost all subjects describe the experience as enlightening, liberating, and personally rewarding.

INDUCING THE OUT-OF-BODY EXPERIENCE

Several strategies have been developed to induce the out-of-body state and to facilitate out-of-body travel. Because sleep appears particularly conducive to out-of-body travel, a procedure called, "Destination Control," was devised to promote OBEs during the sleep state.

DESTINATION CONTROL

Step 1   *Mental Intent.* The objective for out-of-body travel is determined, and the intent to travel out-of-body is clearly formulated. The destination can be either specified or left indefinite.

Step 2   *Pre-sleep Affirmation.* This step is designed to pave the way for out-of-body travel through affirmations presented to the inner self just prior to falling asleep. To delay sleep while affirmations are presented, the Finger-Spread Technique is recommended. The technique requires simply spreading the fingers of either hand and holding the tense-spread position. Suggested affirmations to induce OBEs are:

> *As I sleep, I can leave my body at will to travel wherever I wish. I will remain in control, and I will be protected as I travel. My out-of-body experiences will enrich and empower my life. I will return to my body at any moment I decide to do so. I am now ready to travel out of my body.*

For unspecified destinations, the Destination Control procedure is ended here by slowly relaxing the hand

and allowing sleep to ensue. For specific destinations, however, the finger-spread position is maintained during the two remaining steps.

Step 3 *Destination Control Imagery.* This step guides the out-of-body experience to a specified destination by allowing a clear, mental image of that destination to emerge and become absorbed as fully as possible. If the destination is unfamiliar, imagery of its location on a globe or map is effective in promoting travel.

Step 4 *Imagery/OBE Fusion.* This final step actually initiates the out-of-body travel experience. As the finger spread is ended by slowly relaxing the fingers, images of the physical body at rest are fused with awareness of floating away from the body and being guided to the desired destination.

OBEs during sleep have reportedly engaged interactions with discarnate dimensions, including visits with historical figures or famous personalities who had made the transition. A student reportedly experienced an out-of-body visit during sleep with Albert Einstein, who presented an array of complicated formulas and calculations to him. Upon awakening, the student immediately recorded Einstein's lecture conclusions in his dream journal as follows: "As you can readily see from our calculations, the form of time as we know it in this place is symptomatically caused by the dominant energy of this plane known as light and can be non-existent or different on other planes determined by the dominant and sub-dominant energy forms."

Another student, enrolled in an OBE seminar, reported traveling out-of-body during sleep to a distant Alabama coastal city, and visiting a friend whom she had not seen in several years. During the visit she noted yellow appliances, white tie-back curtains, and a fresh arrangement of red tulips on the counter in her friend's newly decorated kitchen. A phone call the following morning verified the details of the out-of-body visit. Perhaps with more study and refinement of strategies that evoke OBEs during sleep, the empowerment potential of this phenomenon for increasing awareness will become recognized more fully.

Other strategies have been designed to facilitate the out-of-body experience during the normal waking state. "Astral Flight" is an OBE-induction procedure that uses physical relaxation along with astral imagery.

ASTRAL FLIGHT

Step 1 *Preliminary Considerations.* A relaxed, semi-prone, or reclining position is recommended for a period of approximately thirty minutes, during which there must be absolutely no distractions.

Step 2 *Physical Relaxation.* Induce deep physical relaxation by mentally scanning the body, identifying areas of tension, and progressively relaxing specific muscle groups. The procedure is facilitated by slowed breathing and peaceful imagery, along with empowering affirmations such as:

> *I am tranquil and serene; I am secure and in control; I am now fully empowered to travel out-of-body.*

Step 3 *Astral Imagery.* A progression of images engages the out-of-body state and directs the travel experience. First, images of the body at rest are formed, with particular attention focused on specific regions of the

body, the position of the body, and the physical setting. Next, mental images of consciousness are generated as a radiant light form separating from the body
and drifting upward. Finally, conscious awareness is
centered in the rising light form, which is then mentally enveloped in a transparent sphere and directed to
float outward to probe distant realities, as the biological body remains at rest. A silver cord is envisioned
connecting the enveloped light form of consciousness
to the physical body.

Step 4   *The Return.* The out-of-body experience ends with
the simple intent to return to the physical body, and
imagery of the enveloping sphere dissolving as the
light form of consciousness re-enters the body. The
procedure is concluded by a brief period of peaceful
reflection and introspection.

Education, forensics, espionage, and psychotherapy are among
the emerging frontiers of contemporary interest in OBEs. In the
educational setting, the out-of-body technique has been experi-
mentally applied as a motivational and skills-development strategy.
An interesting example of that application was a college art class
that used out-of-body travel to gather artistic ideas. Similarly, a college drama group used the technique as a strategy for improving
acting skills. The out-of-body experience in these academic situations tended to release the flow of creative energy and improve the
quality of creative expression.

The application of OBEs in forensics has centered primarily on
the investigative effort. The technique has been particularly useful as
a strategy for locating missing persons and gathering criminal evidence. Although this application remains speculative and
experimental, the cumulative instances of success suggest many
possibilities for this technique as a valuable investigative tool.

A potentially darker side of OBEs is their intelligence gathering and espionage applications. The out-of-body technique has intriguing potential for acquiring classified data and monitoring secret military and research activities. Out-of-body experts reportedly have been used routinely by some governments for scientific research and intelligence purposes. Through her out-of-body experiences, a physicist with extraordinary psychic skills reportedly assembled a wealth of important scientific data depicting highly advanced technology. Notwithstanding many troublesome ethical issues, governments of the future will, in all probability, continue to explore out-of-body strategies for espionage and research purposes.

Only recently have we begun serious consideration of the therapeutic applications of the out-of-body experience. In instances of severe mental distress, therapeutically managed OBEs can facilitate a more rapid recovery, particularly from disorders such as clinical depression and debilitating stress. A patient undergoing treatment for depression reported that, in the out-of-body state, "I was my old self again." The experience gave him the essential therapeutic support he needed to affirm his potential for complete recovery. Along a similar line, OBEs are sometimes instrumental in promoting recovery from grief. A businessman reported an unusual out-of-body experience in which he visited his recently deceased father in a dimension he described as "filled with light." He embraced his father and at that moment recalled, "I felt complete peace."

SUMMARY

A better understanding of the out-of-body state, its purposes, and its experiences, is important because the phenomenon not only offers new explanations of behavior, it also suggest new frontiers of experience and self-empowerment possibilities. In transcending biological nature, OBEs can effectively engage a liberated state of freedom from biological baggage, thus suggesting unlimited expression of non-biological being. With the physical barriers removed and our mental faculties permitted unrestricted expression, it is not surprising that heightened psychic functions often characterize the out-of-body state. The new insight and expanded awareness resulting from OBEs can increase our knowledge base, while at the same time inspiring and motivating us to overcome growth barriers and achieve new levels of self-fulfillment. The out-of-body experience can suggest solutions to personal problems and provide strategic withdrawal from painful realities, during which we can muster our empowering resources. Perhaps most importantly, OBEs can increase our understanding of ourselves and the nature of our existence in the universe.

OBEs are reflections of our claim to permanence in the universe as a conscious entity, and the absolute survival of our personal identity beyond mere biological existence. To experience the out-of-body state is to experience, although in limited and emblematic form, the transition to a liberated, empowered state of discarnate enrichment. The underlying message of the out-of-body state is the conclusion:

I am immortal.

THE PEAK EXPERIENCE

∽16∽

Oliver Wendell Holmes observed, "A moment's insight is sometimes worth a life's experience." The peak experience, a typically brief but profoundly meaningful event, can provide a flash of insight that can permanently empower our lives. Many advances in science, philosophy, and religion are attributed to the peak experience, in which important new insight and knowledge emerged. The fact that many turning points in history were related to the peak experiences of great men and women, reflects the remarkable empowering potential of this phenomenon.

The peak experience can range from simple experiences such as inspiring encounters with nature, to complex and profoundly significant interactions with higher dimensions that transform and transcend our lives. The peak experience can enlighten and motivate us to reach for greatness. It can give us hope in times of despair, reassurance in times of uncertainty, comfort in times of grief, and safety in times of danger. It can help us to better understand who we are and what we can become. It can engage our highest faculties in a riveting growth event.

The peak experience often occurs when we are at our wit's end, or when we encounter mortality at a deeply personal level. When we are faced with such crises, the peak experience can be a channel of comfort and growth. This was illustrated by a student who was faced with the imminent death of her terminally ill mother. During an overnight visit with her comatose mother in the hospital, she saw a glowing image of a figure wearing a turban-like headdress, standing at her mother's beside. She watched the luminous image, and felt peaceful serenity permeate the room. Soon the image faded, but the serenity lingered as the night wore on. Near dawn, her mother awoke from the coma and, turning toward her daughter, inquired with a smile, "Did you see that wonderful visitor?" She paused, then continued, "He was wearing a turban." With that, she closed her eyes and peacefully made the transition. With calm assurance, the daughter accepted her mother's transition, not as an ending of life, but as the beginning of another beautiful dimension. As Sir Walter Lodge put it, "Death is not a foe, but an inevitable adventure." Like the initiation rites of many mystical orders, death can be perceived as an empowering gateway from one level of attainment to another.

The peak experience often engages our natural surroundings as channels of empowering energies: a snow-blanketed countryside, a towering tree that seems to pierce heaven, or a majestic mountain range. For a journalist, stricken with grief from the recent loss of his wife and infant son in a plane crash, the healing couriers were simply a doe and her fawn. Driving at dusk through the mountains, with the almost intolerable intensity of his loss weighing on his mind, he saw the deer at a distance grazing peacefully along the roadside. As he neared them, he marveled at their grace and beauty. Suddenly, they stood erect, then leaped into the sanctuary of the deep forest. Instantly, he thought of his wife and son, not in some state of distant nothingness, but together in the sanctuary of another magnificent dimension. He felt an almost imperceptible tug at his grief, then quiet release and peaceful acceptance.

For a young engineer, the peak experience was a spectacular sunset that signaled the turning point in his recovery from the death of his wife in an automobile crash. Sitting at dusk on the back deck of his home, he watched the sun disappear behind a bank of clouds. In the gathering darkness, he felt anew the pain of his loss and the overwhelming emptiness in his life. Suddenly, the bank of clouds began to break apart and spread out in ribbons of color over the western horizon, while shafts of sunlight formed fan-like patterns across the sky. As the earth and sky became bathed in a golden radiance, he sensed the weight of his grief being gently lifted, as if drawn by some unseen force behind the magnificent display of light. He felt the despair dissolving away, then gently being replaced by serenity and peace. Lingering on the deck as darkness enveloped the earth, he saw a star shining in the still-glowing sky. He thought of his wife, the star of his heart, but instead of emptiness, he sensed the energies of his being soaring and merging with the energies of a larger, more powerful dimension, revealing a new awareness of the meaning of life and death.

The peak experience is not limited to the crucial issues of life and death; it can involve commonplace, everyday events that inspire and enrich our lives. It can consist simply of a loving memory that engenders inner peace. It can spring from experiences such as walking in a forest or strolling on a beach, encountering the wondrous energies of nature. It can be simply a raised awareness of our oneness with the universe.

SUMMARY

Among our most unique characteristics as human beings is our capacity for empowering experiences that raise our consciousness and transcend our lives. Each peak experience contributes in its own way to that never-ending process.

CONCLUSION

Only in recent years have we begun the serious exploration of the empowering nature of psychic phenomena, yet already we are struck with awe by the expanding body of convincing evidence. No longer can we dismiss the psychic event as merely an incredible, mystical phenomenon with little relevance to post-modern life. The more we probe the psychic world, the more we recognize its magnificent empowering possibilities.

Psychic empowerment goes beyond a simple belief in psychic phenomena: it involves a command of knowledge that justifies that belief and empowering skills that give it validity. Acquiring such knowledge and skills requires an accurate and critical assessment of the psychic experience and its empowering potential. When we evaluate the evidence, we come face to face with certain clear, inescapable conclusions: 1. The mind is unsurpassed in complexity and inexhaustible in potential. We have, at best, merely scratched the surface and tinkered at the borders; 2. The powers of the mind are, for the most part, underdeveloped. Among the mind's most neglected resources are the psychic potentials; 3. Our psychic potentials can be accessed, activated, and developed to empower our lives and bring forth global change; 4. A spark of divine power exists in everyone. Psychic empowerment fans that spark and brings it alive to illuminate our lives with a clearer awareness of our destiny for greatness and permanence in the universe.

Psychic self-empowerment is an endless process of growth, discovery, and change. Its hallmark is a recognition of human worth, a firm commitment to truth, and a deep awareness of the illimitable Power within each of us. Ultimately, psychic empowerment brings us, individually and collectively, into oneness with that Power.

PART
THREE

The Seven-Day
Psychic Empowerment Plan

THE PLAN

The techniques of psychic empowerment are available to everyone. They can be used to enrich our lives, promote our personal success, and bring forth change in the world. Because psychic development is a natural, spontaneous process, even sporadic empowerment efforts will yield empowering benefits; but the full realization of our psychic potentials requires an organized approach which recognizes the basic principles of psychic development, and the human capacity to achieve a state of full psychic empowerment.

The Seven-Day Psychic Empowerment Plan is designed to activate our inner psychic empowerment potentials and initiate a psychic-empowered lifestyle, which can continue to evolve through the systematic practice of empowering strategies. The plan organizes the concepts of psychic empowerment into a structure which progresses from simple affirmations to more complex psychic activation strategies. Techniques discussed earlier in the book are now presented as part of a plan to promote heightened psychic awareness and empowerment.

DAY ONE

The psychic-empowerment goal for day one is twofold: first, to build a state of self-esteem and personal worth; and second, to generate a state of psychic growth readiness. The most direct and effective technique for achieving that goal is Positive Self-talk. Through positive self-talk which affirms our self-worth and personal adequacy, an empowering interaction within the self is initiated. The result is an empowered state of well-being and maximum growth readiness. Beginning upon awakening and continuing at frequent intervals throughout the day, empowering self-talk is engaged either mentally or verbally as follows:

I am a person of worth.

Success is my destiny.

I am empowered to achieve my goals.

I am capable and secure.

I am prepared to meet the challenges of life.

I believe in myself and the unlimited power within my being.

I am tranquil and secure.

I am at peace with myself and the universe.

I am surrounded by boundless opportunities for growth and self-discovery.

My life is filled with purpose.

I am resolved to enrich my own life and to help make the world a better place.

These are only examples of effective empowering self-talk, which can be supplemented by more specific self-empowering suggestions. Positive self-talk is critical to our psychic empowerment, and is recommended as a daily component of the seven-day plan.

DAY TWO

The goal for day two is to build imagery skills considered critical to psychic empowerment. Mental imagery gives empowering substance to positive self-talk, and enables us to interact with the innermost part of the self to activate our highest psychic potentials. Even those psychic faculties residing in subconscious regions of the mind are responsive to empowering mental imagery.

Two visualization exercises are introduced in day two of our plan. Included are the Dream Recall Strategy and the Regressive Imagery Procedure, which are practice exercises for developing our mental imagery skills.

DREAM RECALL STRATEGY

This strategy is practiced immediately upon awakening, and is useful not only in building our imagery skills, but also for improving our memory and understanding of our dreams.

Step 1   Select a particularly vivid dream experience, perhaps a recurrent dream.

Step 2   Mentally recreate the dream experience to include clear images, paying particular attention to specific details and dream actions.

Step 3 Involve yourself in the dream-recall experience. If possible, become an active participant in the recreated dream images and action.

Step 4 Allow the dream recall experience to become increasingly vivid. Let yourself flow with the experience.

Step 5 Conclude the exercise with powerful, positive affirmations of your psychic potential.

REGRESSIVE IMAGERY PROCEDURE

This strategy is an excellent practice technique for exercising our mental imagery powers and stimulating creativity. The procedure requires a quiet setting and approximately thirty minutes.

Step 1 Assume a relaxed, tranquil state of mind and, with your eyes closed, recall some past, rewarding experience in as much detail as possible. Experiences with nature are recommended: perhaps a walk in a forest, a mountain climb, a summer thunderstorm, an inspiring sunrise, or a tranquil moonlit cove.

Step 2 Mentally recreate the experience and envision it as fully as possible. Notice details such as movement, color, and sound.

Step 3 Focus on your feelings as you envision the experience. Allow yourself to relive the experience, interact with it, and absorb its peacefulness and tranquillity.

Step 4 Mentally travel back in time to an even earlier experience, perhaps your very earliest memory or a pleasant experience for which recall is sketchy. Project your awareness to that situation and note in detail the characteristics of the experience.

Step 5 Enlarge your vision of the experience by filling in the missing images and creating new pictures in your mind. Immerse yourself in the experience. Allow your creative imagery to flow spontaneously, infusing your mind with the scene's peaceful tranquillity.

Step 6 Allow the imagery experience to run its course, then before opening your eyes, affirm:

> *I am now empowered to use my psychic resources. Whatever I now choose to imagine can become my reality.*

The Dream Recall Strategy and Regressive Imagery Procedure are recommended as daily practice exercises for the remaining five days of the psychic empowerment plan.

DAY THREE

Day three introduces two procedures designed to induce physical relaxation while evoking a state of both psychic and generalized empowerment. The Finger Interlocking Technique is a quick, three-step process that can be performed almost anywhere. The Therapeutic Relaxation Induction Procedure (TRIP) is a composite of several empowering techniques, including physical relaxation, positive affirmations, mental imagery, and a unique attunement exercise. The TRIP takes a little longer, about thirty minutes, to complete. Both procedures can be practiced as often as desired during the balance of the seven-day plan.

Finger Interlocking Technique

Step 1   Take a few deep breaths, exhaling slowly.

Step 2   Join the thumb and middle finger of each hand.

Step 3   Bring the hands together to form interlocking circles with your thumbs and middle fingers. Relax both hands as you give yourself the affirmation:

> *I am now completely relaxed. My body is in a state of complete balance. I am protected, tranquil, and serene.*

This technique not only generates a relaxed physical state, but protects the psychic energy system from depletion. In that temporarily closed psychic state, new psychic energies can be generated through the simple affirmation:

> *I am now energized with abundant power.*

Therapeutic Relaxation Induction Procedure (TRIP)

Settle back and let yourself become as comfortable and relaxed as possible. Slow your breathing and develop a relaxed, rhythmic breathing pattern, taking a little longer to exhale. As you clear your mind, close your eyes and continue to focus your attention on your breathing. You are now ready to begin the TRIP.

Step 1   *Wrinkled Brow Rejuvenation Release.* Tighten the muscles in your forehead and between your eyes, then very slowly relax them. Follow the relaxation as it spreads into the muscles of your forehead, around your eyes, over your face, and into your neck and shoulders. Feel the release of rejuvenating energy as it permeates the muscles of your forehead and spreads downward.

Step 2   *Shoulder Lift.* Lift your shoulders and tighten the muscles as you hold them in the lift position. Now slowly relax the muscles and let your shoulders return to normal, as you count from one to three. On the count of three, let the relaxation spread deeply into your chest and downward into your arms.

Step 3   *Finger Spread.* Spread the fingers of both hands and hold the spread position as you notice the tightness in the muscles of your hands and lower arms. Now slowly relax the muscles in your fingers and hands as you allow the relaxation to soak into the joints and muscles of your hands and arms. Notice the pleasant tingling in your hands as the energy spreads right out through the tips of your fingers.

Step 4   *Abdominal Tuck.* Tuck in and tighten the muscles in your abdomen. Hold the tightened position for a few moments, then slowly relax the muscles. Notice the relaxation soaking into the muscles, going deeper and deeper into the pit of your stomach.

Step 5   *Knee Press.* Press your knees together very tightly. Hold them in the pressed position until you begin to tire, then slowly relax. You will notice the relaxation spreading above and below your knees. Let the relaxation go deeper and deeper into the muscles and joints of your legs.

Step 6   *Toe Lift.* For this step, you may wish to remove your shoes. Lift your toes upward and hold them in the lift position as you notice the tension in your feet and ankles. Now slowly relax your toes, allowing them to return to the normal position. Notice the relaxation in your ankles, feet, and right into the tips of your toes.

Step 7   *Attunement Activation.* Allow peaceful, spontaneous imagery to flow gently in and out of your mind. Notice the color, movement, and detail of the imagery, but do not attempt to arrest it. At this stage, simply allow the images to come and go spontaneously.

From among the images flowing through your mind, select one that seems right for you at the moment and focus all of your attention on it. Become so absorbed with the image that you lose yourself in the experience. Stay with the image until you have fully absorbed its energies.

Finally, let the imagery dissolve away until nothing remains. Your mind is now emptied of all active thought. The systems of your being are now neutralized, synchronized, and balanced inwardly and outwardly. Allow the attunement state to continue effortlessly.

Step 8   *Empowerment Affirmation.* The procedure is concluded with the following affirmation:

> *I am now fully attuned inwardly and outwardly. My total being is infused with powerful, positive energy. I am empowered to activate my potentials and achieve my highest goals. The energies of growth are now unleashed to flow throughout my total being.*

DAY FOUR

The psychic empowerment activities for day four are designed to promote development of our telepathic sending and receiving skills. Our telepathic mechanisms are seldom, if ever, totally inactive; but for the most part, telepathy is spontaneous and uncontrolled. Through practice, we can develop our telepathic powers and organize our sending and receiving mechanisms into a functional communication system. To achieve that important goal, day four introduces the Telepathic Activation Procedure (TAP). The three-step procedure is designed to facilitate a mental and physical state conducive to both sending and receiving psychic messages.

TELEPATHIC ACTIVATION PROCEDURE

Step 1   For either sending or receiving, clear your mind while relaxing your physical body. An excellent mind-clearing and relaxation technique combines imagery of a clear, blue sky with the affirmation:

> *I am now becoming relaxed as my mind becomes*
> *clear and free of active thought.*

The clearing and relaxation process is further facilitated by breathing slowly, and mentally scanning the body from the head down. Areas of tension are noted and muscles relaxed.

Step 2   For telepathic sending, formulate the telepathic message and generate related imagery. Visualize a vehicle, such as a transparent sphere, for transporting the thought message. Actively concentrate all thought on the message and related imagery. Release the telepathic message to go forth to the envisioned target receiver.

Step 3   For telepathic receiving, maintain a mentally passive
state and allow the thought messages and images to
emerge into conscious awareness.

In addition to its application in person-to-person telepathy, this
procedure can be applied on a global scale for sending telepathic
messages of global significance. For that application, the earth is
envisioned as the target receiver and the message is sent forth as a
light form. Examples of global telepathy are messages of peace, harmony, and good will dispersed as a band of light encircling the earth.

DAY FIVE

Like other forms of ESP, precognitive skills can be acquired through
practice and experience. Day five of our psychic empowerment
plan introduces two strategies designed to develop our precognitive powers. The first of these strategies, a procedure called Doors,
emphasizes our powers of choice and our capacity to intervene in
future events. The four-step procedure requires a quiet setting and
a period of approximately twenty minutes.

THE DOORS PROCEDURE

Step 1   While in a relaxed, tranquil state, envision a wall with
many doors and the word "Future" boldly inscribed on
the wall. Creatively imagine doors of many colors and
materials: gold, steel, wood, glass, silver, brass, and
jade. Imagine a word representing the future inscribed
on each door. Examples of possible inscriptions are
career, finances, relationships, family, and health. The
inscriptions can be deeply personal, like the names of

people, or they can be national or global in nature. Allow one door to remain without an inscription.

Step 2   Select a door and envision yourself opening it. Allow a panoramic view of the future to emerge. You may choose to step through the door and become an active participant in the unfolding events of the future.

Step 3   Select other doors as preferred and open them at will. The non-inscribed door is used to reveal future events such as natural catastrophes, political incidents, and civil disasters.

Step 4   Conclude the procedure with affirmations of your power to use precognitive knowledge responsibly to influence the future or to cope effectively with unalterable future events.

PRECOGNITIVE REVIEW

The second precognitive strategy for day five is Precognitive Review. While essentially a practice exercise for building precognitive skills, the procedure is particularly effective in exploring the future of personal issues, including relationships and career concerns.

Step 1   Identify a situation for which precognitive information would be useful.

Step 2   Realistically envision the prevailing situation, giving attention to specific details.

Step 3   Mentally enumerate the potential outcomes of the present situation. Identify as many alternatives as possible.

Step 4   Review the potential outcomes, turning them over one by one in your mind. Permit other outcomes to unfold mentally. Allow this process to continue until a particular outcome emerges as the strongest or most probable.

Step 5 Following a brief rest period in which the mind is cleared, repeat steps three and four, giving particular attention to any confirmation of the previous results.

Step 6 Continue the review process until a clear impression of the future unfolds. Document your results.

Both strategies for day five are designed to exercise the mind's critical precognitive processes, while at the same time accessing specific precognitive knowledge.

DAY SIX

Day six introduces exercises designed to develop our clairvoyant powers. Clairvoyant impressions often consist of vivid images that depict meaningful realities. Consequently, strategies designed to develop clairvoyant skills typically emphasize creativity and imagery powers. Among the most effective of these strategies is the following six-step meditation procedure that exercises the "third eye," a theoretical imagery faculty associated with clairvoyance.

THE THIRD EYE EXERCISE

Step 1 Induce a relaxed state, using such techniques as body scan, relaxing imagery, and slowed breathing.

Step 2 With the eyes closed, envision a smooth, glass-like plane void of disruptive structures.

Step 3 Imagine a myriad of glowing geometric structures—spheres, obelisks, cubes, and pyramids—rising above the plane.

Step 4 Focus on the structures and allow images to emerge as if projected on the structures' surfaces.

Step 5 From among the various images, select a particularly relevant one and allow a progressive, spontaneous unfolding of new images.

Step 6 Mentally create a dominant structure to function as a clairvoyant screen, and project upon it the critical elements of a current situation for which additional information is sought. Allow new information to unfold on the screen as clairvoyant images.

Like other psychic faculties, clairvoyance improves with practice. Activities involving familiar materials and everyday situations have been highly effective in building clairvoyant skills. In addition to the preceding third-eye exercise, the following practice activities are recommended for day six:

- Guess the hour before checking the time.

- Pull a book at random from a shelf and guess its total number of pages.

- Draw a card from a shuffled deck and guess its identity.

- Guess the amount of change in your pocket or purse.

These are simple activities, but with repeated practice, their empowering benefits can be pronounced.

DAY SEVEN

The Seven-Day Psychic Empowerment Plan is concluded with the powerful meditative strategy, Ascending the Pyramid. This exercise combines imagery and empowering affirmations in a step-by-step procedure that culminates in a riveting infusion of power. It requires approximately ten minutes, and is initiated by slowed breathing and relaxation, in which the mind is cleared, followed by imagery of a pyramid with ten steps leading to its apex. The ten steps, each with an inscription, are envisioned one-by-one, beginning at the first step and culminating at the top of the pyramid, as appropriate empowering affirmations are given.

Ascending the Pyramid

Step 1   *Love.*

> *Love is basic to my life. It is the energizing foundation of my existence and the center of my being. In my capacity to love, I discover myself and other human beings. Love is the most powerful expression of my being.*

Step 2   *Forgiveness.*

> *In forgiving myself and others, I unblock the flow of growth potential in my life. Forgiveness is the attitude that characterizes myself and my interactions with others. It is the transforming inner force that soars always upward toward harmony and peace.*

Step 3 *Peace.*

> *Peace is the river that flows through my being. It is deep, abiding, and secure. Infused with inner peace, I can weather any storm that enters my life. Disappointments, misfortune, and uncertainties all yield to the quieting force of inner peace.*

Step 4 *Faith.*

> *Faith is the elevating, activating power in my life. It is my belief in the divine power within my own being. It is the essence of my existence in the universe. In adversity, faith sustains and upholds me. It reveals boundless possibilities for the present and larger dimensions of meaning for the future. Faith is the eternal substance of triumphant living.*

Step 5 *Choice.*

> *Each moment of my life, I am choosing. I choose to think or not to think, to act or not to act, to feel or not to feel. Because I choose, I am responsible for my thoughts, actions, and feelings. They are all mine, and I choose to own them. I am what I choose to be at any moment in time.*

Step 6 *Change.*

> *Change is the current of growth and progress. To become more vibrant, full of life, sincere, and compassionate are all are changes I value. Positive change carries me always forward to experience something new and vital about myself each day.*

Step 7 *Awareness.*

> *Through expanded awareness, my life is enriched and the meaning of my existence is clarified. As I become more aware of my inner self, I become more completely attuned to my being. I know myself best when I come face to face with the totality of my existence in the here and now.*

Step 8 *Knowledge.*

> *Knowledge is power. Through knowing my inner self, I gain power over my life and my destiny. Knowledge empowers me to function more productively and to engage the future more effectively. Given knowledge, whatever its source, I am empowered to bring about needed change in myself and the world.*

Step 9 *Balance.*

> *Balance in my life enables me to be spontaneous and free. My thoughts, feelings, and actions are integrated into a harmonious system that empowers me to adapt to life's demands and to liberate my highest potentials.*

Step 10 *Empowerment.*

> *In my capacity to love, forgive, experience peace, exercise faith, make choices, promote change, expand awareness, discover knowledge, and maintain balance, I am fully empowered each moment of my life.*

The empowering effects of Ascending the Pyramid can be magnified by envisioning oneself pausing at the pyramid's apex and reflecting on the experience. During that reflective period, any of the preceding affirmations can be reaffirmed, and additional affirmations and related imagery can be introduced. The procedure, along with our Seven-Day Psychic Empowerment Plan, is concluded with the simple affirmation:

I AM EMPOWERED.

APPENDIX
DREAM SYMBOLS

The interpretative significance of a dream symbol depends on a number of factors; among them, the nature of the dream itself, and the dreamer's personal characteristics, past experiences, and prevailing life circumstances. Despite these influencing variables, the meanings of many dream symbols appear to be reasonably stable. The purpose of this glossary is not to constrict the potential meanings of dreams, but to expand the interpretative possibilities of dream symbols, and to illustrate the potential value of dreams in promoting our personal insight and growth.

abyss. Emptiness or the unknown. "Falling into an abyss" suggests despair and feelings of hopelessness.

accident. The unexpected; loss of innocence or opportunity. Accidents suggest the importance of planning, foresight, caution, and critical assessment of current circumstances.

acrobat. Free, uninhibited, playful, and happy.

animal. The characteristics typically attributed to certain animals are often symbolized by the animal. The dove will often symbolize peace; the cat, independence; the dog, friendliness; and the bear, aggression. A dream of a struggle with an animal can symbolize a threatening impulse, whereas a dream of stroking a pet can represent our need to nurture.

auditorium. The social self. An empty auditorium can represent constricted social interests, whereas a crowded auditorium suggests a need for social interaction.

avalanche. Urgency, future adversity, a need for immediate action.

badge. Courage, honor, or striving for integrity.

banner. Future achievement, success, or unexpected recognition.

barn. Practicality, basic needs, or a simple lifestyle.

bird. Aspiration, drive for self-fulfillment, or the human spirit. A specific bird can represent a particular characteristic or preferred course of action. The eagle symbolizes power and suggests dominance; the sparrow, a carefree spirit; the hawk, aggression; the blue bird, happiness and enduring relationships; and the red bird, passion and impulsiveness.

bridge. Transition, change, new opportunity, or desire for continuity.

butterfly. Change, spiritual growth, and vulnerability.

candle. Truth, wisdom, and intelligence.

cavern. Mystery, desire to explore the unknown, or creativity.

chase. Escape, competitiveness, or vulnerability.

classroom. Opportunity, growth, or the desire to control or to be controlled.

color. Typically creativity; however the particular color can have special significance. Red represents emotional intensity, anger, and urgency; pink, tenderness, femininity, and sensitivity; yellow, warmth and friendliness; green, virility, health, and wealth; light blue, peace and serenity; deep blue, the unknown and possible danger; orange, unpredictable circumstances; purple, mystery and spirituality; white, purity; gray, conservatism; black, unyielding or danger; and brown, practicality.

construction. A new beginning, new interests, changing relationships, or new projects.

conversation. Desire for social closeness, the need for acceptance.

crying. Guilt, insecurity, or the need to undo.

fire. Passion, a desire for vengeance, aggression, or a destroyed relationship.

firearm. Self-destruction, hostility, aggression, desperation, recklessness, or danger.

fish. Evasiveness, resistance, or the need to escape.

flood. Being overwhelmed, caught off guard, unprepared, vulnerable.

flower. Serenity and pleasure. Specific flowers can convey a particular message or denote a specific characteristic or need. Roses are associated with affection and the expression of love; pansies, temporary but intense relationship; sweet pea, children or the desire to have children; carnation, a pensive, reflective state of mind; chrysanthemum, a gala affair; orchid, permanence and commitment; petunia, rugged endurance; daffodil, warmth or the restoration of a relationship; tulip, productivity; hyacinth, reflection and a time to nurture relationships; gardenia, sensuality, persuasive powers; golden rod, abundance and security; violets, maturity and logic; and mixed flowers, balance and harmony within the self.

flying. Freedom or possibly an out-of-body experience.

fog. Uncertainty, unpreparedness, and procrastination. To be enveloped in fog suggests shortsightedness or danger.

fortress. The self's defense system; hence a crumbling fortress symbolizes vulnerability.

fruit. Productivity, the desire for children, or an intimate relationship.

holiday. Change, freedom, escape, or travel.

horse. Power or control.

house. Family and social relationships.

ice. A cold relationship, inflexibility, shallow emotions, unwise investments, or a stalemate.

infant. A new beginning, regression tendencies, or innocence.

injury. Vulnerability, traumatic experience, weakness, depleted power resources, threatened personal security, inferiority feelings, or arrested growth.

island. Refuge, safety, or security.

jewel/jewelry. Enrichment, good fortune, and certain characteristics of the self depending on the nature of the item: The diamond signifies commitment and resolution; the ruby, quality and depth; the topaz, sincerity and warmth; the pearl, moral and spiritual values; the amethyst, devotion; gold, integrity; and silver, maturity.

kissing. Desire for closeness, self love, or erotic desire.

ladder. Desire to excel, ambition, or growth.

lantern. Self orientation, skepticism, limited insight, or constricted interests.

laughter. Self-acceptance or self-satisfaction.

letter. Conscious or subconscious interaction, inner-attunement, forthcoming insight, or responsiveness to new knowledge.

light. A bright light signifies enlightenment and understanding. A flash of light symbolizes sudden insight.

metal. Metal objects can signify some unyielding aspect of the personality. Gold represents striving for either purity or wealth; silver represents excellence; and steel indicates fixed beliefs or inflexibility. Metal that becomes pliable in the dream suggests a willingness to modify one's position.

money. Material interests or financial concerns. A profitable financial venture is symbolized by finding money, whereas financial reversal is revealed by losing money. Large sums of money and counting money symbolize success.

monster. Inner fears, insecurities, struggle, or vulnerability.

moon. Romance, fantasy, mystery, strength, or sincerity.

mountain. Personal growth, obstacle, challenge, or struggle to achieve goals.

music. Harmony, balance, and inner peace.

nudity. Vulnerability, inferiority feelings, and inadequacy.

ocean. Typically, the ocean symbolizes the subconscious. A turbulent ocean suggests personal upheaval, inner struggle, discontent, and restlessness; whereas calm seas represent balance and harmony within the self.

painting. As a dream activity, painting represents an attempt to reverse some past action or to correct an adverse situation. Viewing a painting suggests passivity and possible voyeuristic impulses.

paralysis. Frustration, fear of failure, or hopelessness.

passageway. Transition, advancement, or escape.

people. Social interests or need for social acceptance. Strangers represent a new situation or the need to be cautious.

physical body. Sexual interests, narcissism, when dreaming of one's own body, or concern for bodily functions and health.

race. Urgency, escape, or the need for patience.

railroad crossing. Caution or impending danger.

rainstorm. Unrequited love, unfilled desires, striving for excitement.

road. Journey, new discoveries, or an important transition.

rocket. Male sexuality, ambition, aggression, or virility concerns.

sanctuary. Safety, spiritual growth, or escape.

ship. Destiny. Steering a ship signifies being in control of destiny, whereas being a passenger suggests others are in control.

shoes. Material, earthly interests.

shopping. Efforts to nurture. Buying clothing represents strivings for acceptance and affiliation; buying shoes represents progress and advancement; buying food represents efforts to satisfy the needs of the inner self; and buying toiletries symbolizes erotic strivings.

singing. Happiness and fulfillment, spontaneity, genuineness, friendliness, or future gain.

skeleton. Impoverishment of personal resources; loss of power, reputation, or status.

skidding. Tendencies toward excessive risk-taking, altercation in a social relationship, or an impulsive confrontation.

snowstorm. Indecisiveness, unpreparedness, or vulnerability.

stairway. Transition, challenge, or struggle.

stone. A stone building symbolizes stability, whereas a stone landscape or boulder represents obstacles, adversity, and resistance.

struggle. Inner conflict, need for achievement, barriers to growth.

sunburn. Vulnerability to external influences, social pressures in particular.

sunrise. The beginning of a new and productive growth stage. A brilliant sunrise denotes unusual growth opportunities. Recurring dreams of a sunrise suggests self-confidence and a readiness to accommodate change and achieve new goals.

theater. Fantasy or escape needs.

tombstone. Gateway, death, or other life transition.

tower. Ambition, independence, self-reliance, male sexuality, strength, and purpose.

train. Spiritual growth, travel, or change.

tree. As a phallic symbol, virility, but when barren, sexual deficiency. A fallen tree can represent defeat, whereas a towering tree can signify aspiration.

uniform. Conformity, authority, or power.

walking. Patience, steady progress, or consistency.

GLOSSARY

apperception. A phenomenon in which sensory perceptions are associated with inner, subjective impressions.

Ascending the Pyramid. A strategy combining imagery of a pyramid and self-affirmations to promote psychic empowerment.

Astral Flight. An imagery and relaxation procedure for inducing out-of-body travel.

astral projection. *See out-of-body experience.*

astral travel. *See out-of-body experience.*

automatic writing. A psychic strategy in which spontaneous or involuntary writing is used to bring forth information, typically from the subconscious mind.

clairvoyance. The psychic perception of objects, conditions, situations, or events.

clairvoyant reversal. A rare phenomenon in which clairvoyant information is revealed in reverse form. Examples are reversed numbers and spellings.

cognitive functions perspective. The view that psychic faculties, including telepathy and other forms of ESP, exist within the cognitive structure of the brain.

collective clairvoyance. The combining of clairvoyant faculties of two or more persons to gather clairvoyant information.

control imagery. Meditation exercise designed to shape the future by generating images of desired developments or outcomes.

Composite Strategy for Telepathy. A two-component strategy for activating telepathic sending and receiving.

crystal gazing. A technique typically using a crystal ball to initiate psychic processes.

Crystal Screen. A technique using various practice articles, along with the crystal ball, for building basic imagery skills required for activating specific forms of ESP.

déjà vu. A phenomenon in which a new event appears familiar or as if it had been previously experienced.

Destination Control. A strategy utilizing sleep to induce out-of-body travel.

Doors. A precognitive strategy that emphasizes choice and self-determination.

dowser. One who practices dowsing.

dowsing. A procedure using rods to access psychic information including, but not limited to subterranean resources.

Dream Recall Strategy. An imagery practice exercise in which past dream experiences are visualized.

ESA. *See extrasensory apperception.*

ESP. *See extrasensory perception.*

extrasensory apperception (ESA). A phenomenon in which sensory perceptions of changes produced in external objects are related to internal psychic elements or faculties to reveal new psychic knowledge. Examples are sand reading and the wrinkled-sheet technique.

extrasensory perception (ESP). The knowledge of, or response to, events, conditions, and situations independently of known sensory mechanisms or processes.

Fingerpad Engagement Procedure. A balancing technique in which the fingerpads of both hands are joined as psychic empowering affirmations are presented.

Finger Interlocking Technique. A three-step strategy designed to induce physical relaxation and inner balance.

Finger Spread Technique. A procedure requiring a spreading of the fingers of either hand and a brief holding of the spread position as empowering affirmations are presented, followed by a slow relaxing of the fingers. The technique is useful as a hypnotic induction strategy as well as sleep arrest strategy.

Focal Shift. A crystal gazing procedure designed to generate a mental state conducive to ESP.

Future Probe Technique. A group procedure designed to access precognitive data.

Future Screen. A precognitive activating strategy emphasizing physical relaxation and imagery.

generalized empowerment self-talk. The use of self-talk to target empowerment to general goals or collective inner functions.

global telepathy. The psychic engagement of a global interaction for such purposes as bringing forth global peace.

NDE. *See near-death experience.*

near-death experience (NDE). An experience in which death appears imminent, often accompanied by a sense of separation of consciousness from the biological body.

numerology. The study of the psychic significance of numbers.

objectology. The study of tangible objects, including psychic tools, and their relationships to psychic events and processes.

OBE. *See out-of-body experience.*

OBE Conditioning Procedure. A five-step procedure for stimulating out-of-body travel during sleep.

out-of-body experience (OBE). A state of awareness in which the locus of perception shifts to result in a conscious sense of being in a spatial location away from the physical body.

out-of-body PK. The human capacity to influence matter or motion while in the out-of-body state. *See psychokinesis.*

Palm Memory Exercise. An imagery skill-building exercise in which the palm is visualized.

Peripheral Glow Procedure. A relaxation and ESP-conditioning exercise requiring eye fixation and expanded peripheral vision.

PK. *See psychokinesis.*

PK Bombardment. A PK procedure that targets mental energies in an effort to influence the fall of a coin.

PK Illumination. An imagery procedure designed to unleash inner rejuvenating energy.

precognition. Extrasensory awareness of the future.

Precognitive Review. A five-step procedure designed to develop precognitive faculties.

pre-sleep suggestion. A strategy in which suggestion designed to influence dreaming is presented immediately prior to sleep.

psychic antithesis. A phenomenon in which psychic materials represent their opposites or direct contrasts.

psychic empowerment. A state of personal power in which inner psychic faculties are used to achieve personal goals and promote personal growth.

psychic empowerment self-talk. The use of self-talk to initiate a self-contained state of psychic empowerment.

psychic star. In the wrinkled-sheet technique, a star appearing among the patterns. This characteristic is often found in the wrinkled sheets of gifted psychics.

psychokinesis (PK). The ability of the mind to influence objects, events, and processes in the apparent absence of intervening physical energy or intermediary instrumentation. An extended definition of PK includes its capacity to influence internal biological systems.

psychometry. The use of tangible objects, typically of a personal nature, to activate psychic functions, particularly clairvoyance.

reality slip. A situational cue that precipitates a precognitive impression.

recurring dream. The repetition of a specific dream without significant change or variation in content.

Regressive Imagery Procedure. An imagery practice strategy in which past experiences are visualized.

Rejuvenation PK. A PK procedure for activating the physical body's rejuvenation potential.

retrocognition. Extrasensory awareness of the past.

sand reading. A procedure using a hand imprint in a tray of sand to facilitate psychic functions.

self-empowerment. A state of personal power originating within the self.

Sequential Imagery Technique. An imagery practice strategy in which pictures or scenes are mentally recreated.

serial clairvoyant dream. A series of clairvoyant dreams that guides the dreamer, often symbolically, around a central theme.

serial dream. A series of dreams in which sequences of information, often precognitive in nature, are set forth.

Sleep Arrest Strategy. A procedure in which sleep is either delayed or arrested in its earliest stages, as suggestions or affirmations are presented.

specific self-talk. The use of self-talk to target empowerment to specific goals or particular psychic faculties.

Spontaneous Future Imagery. A meditation exercise designed to access the future by envisioning a mental screen upon which future events unfold.

Strategic Telepathic Procedure. A procedure designed to promote telepathy through instruction, practice, and guided learning.

table tilting. A group procedure that employs a small table to access psychic knowledge.

Telepathic Activation Procedure (TAP). A three-step procedure for activating telepathic sending and receiving.

telepathy. The psychic sending and receiving of cognitive and affective contents.

Therapeutic Relaxation Induction Procedure (TRIP). A progressive relaxation strategy designed to reduce excessive stress and evoke a state of generalized empowerment.

third eye. A mental faculty associated with clairvoyance, connected to the sixth chakra, located at the center of the forehead.

toe lift technique. A three-step strategy designed to induce physical relaxation.

TRIP. *See Therapeutic Relaxation Induction Procedure.*

two-component disengagement principle. The concept that out-of-body experiences occur in the disengagement of two systems, one biological and the other astral or extrabiological.

Wellness Activation Strategy. A strategy designed to activate the PK potential to generate and distribute wellness throughout the physical body.

wrinkled sheet technique. A technique utilizing a crumpled sheet of paper to facilitate psychic processes.

SUGGESTED READINGS

⤷

The study of psychic phenomena is an integration of various psychodynamic psychologies, humanistic psychology, and the more recent cognitive and transpersonal systems. Many writers have contributed to this emerging force in the study of human behavior that increasingly recognizes the role of higher planes and advanced cognitive faculties in personal empowerment. Rather than trying to be comprehensive, this list represents only a sampling of writings of various traditions, each of which is incorporated, though at times only indirectly, within the post-modern empowerment perspective.

Adler, A. *Superiority and Social Interests: A Collection of Later Writing.* Evanston: Northwestern University Press, 1964.

Allport, G. *Becoming.* New Haven: Yale University Press, 1955.

Berger, A. *The Aristocracy of the Dead: New Findings in Postmortem Survival.* Jefferson: McFarland, 1987.

Bergland, R. *The Fabric of Mind.* New York: Penguin, 1986.

Cousins, N. *Head First: The Biology of Hope and the Healing Power of the Mind.* New York: Penguin, 1989.

Cranston, S. and C. Williams. *Reincarnation: A New Horizon in Science, Religion, and Society.* New York: Julian Press, 1984.

Curtis, R., ed. *Self-defeating Behaviors: Experimental Research, Clinical Impressions, and Practical Implications.* New York: Plenum, 1989.

DiMatteo, M. *The Psychology of Health, Illness and Medical Care: An Individual Perspective.* Florence: Brooks/Cole, 1991.

Edge, H., et. al. *Foundations of Parapsychology: Exploring the Boundaries of Human Capacity.* New York: Routledge & Kegan Paul, 1986.

Ehrenwald, J. *The ESP Experience: A Psychiatric Validation.* New York: Basic Books, 1978.

Frankl, V. *The Doctor and the Soul.* New York: Knopf, 1955.

———. *Psychotherapy and Existentialism.* New York: Washington Square Press, 1967.

———. *The Will to Meaning: Foundations and Applications of Logotherapy.* New York: Penguin, 1988.

French, T. M. and Erika Fromm. *Dream Interpretation: A New Approach.* New York: Penguin, 1964.

Freud, S. *Collected Papers.* North Pomfret: Hogarth, 1956.

———. *An Outline of Psychoanalysis.* New York: Norton, 1949.

Fromm, E. *The Sane Society.* New York: Rinehart, 1955.

———. *The Heart of Man.* Glenview: Harper and Collins, 1964.

Fromm, E. and R. Shor. *Hypnosis: Research Developments and Perspectives.* 2nd ed. Chicago: Aldine-Atherton, 1979.

Fromm, E. and S. Kahn. *Self-hypnosis: The Chicago Paradigm.* New York: Guilford, 1990.

Gardner, J. *Self Renewal.* Glenview: Harper & Collins, 1964.

Goleman, D. and D. Heller. *The Pleasures of Psychology.* New York: Penguin, 1986.

Hall, J. *Hypnosis: A Jungian Perspective.* New York: Guilford, 1989.

Horney, K. *Self-analysis.* New York: Norton.

———. *Neurosis and Human Growth.* New York: Norton, 1950.

Jung, C. G. *Modern Man in Search of a Soul*. Niles: Harcourt, 1953.

———. *The Undiscovered Self*. London: Kegan Paul, 1958.

Kleinke, C. *Coping with Life Challenges*. Florence: Brooks/Cole, 1991.

Locke, S. and D. Colligan. *The Healer Within: The New Medicine of Mind and Body*. New York: Penguin, 1987.

Maslow, A. *Religions, Values, and Peak-Experiences*. Columbus: The Ohio State University Press, 1964.

———. *Toward a Psychology of Being*. New York: Van Norstrand Reinhold, 1968.

May, R. et. al., ed. *Existence*. New York: Basic Books, 1958.

Mindell, A. *Working on Yourself Alone: Inner Dreambody Work*. New York: Penguin, 1990.

Ornstein, R. *The Psychology of Consciousness*. New York: Penguin, 1986.

Perry, J., ed. *Personal Identity*. Berkley: University of California Press, 1975.

Rhine, J. B. *New World of the Mind*. New York: William Sloane, 1953.

———. *The Reach of the Mind*. New York: William Morrow, 1973.

Rhine, L. *Something Hidden*. Jefferson: McFarland, 1983.

Rogers, C. *On Becoming a Person*. Burlington: Houghton Mifflin, 1961.

Sanders, S. *Clinical Self-Hypnosis: The Power of Words and Images*. New York: Guilford, 1990.

Shekerjian, D. *Uncommon Genius: How Great Ideas are Born*. New York: Penguin, 1990.

Slate, J. *Psychic Phenomena: New Principles, Techniques and Applications*. Jefferson: McFarland, 1988.

Speigel, H. and D. Speigel. *Trance and Treatment: Clinical Use of Hypnosis*. Washington: American Psychiatric Press, 1987.

Tillich, P. *The Courage to Be*. New Haven: Yale University Press, 1952.

INDEX

PSYCHIC SENSE
Training and Developing Psychic Sensitivity
by Mary Swainson and Louisa Bennett

As new energies infiltrate the planet, causing expanded awareness, more and more people have found themselves opening up to their inner psychic powers. Many do not know how to productively develop these often startling phenomena. This book is an answer to that need.

Psychic Sense describes the training process and subsequent realization of the successful medium. Mary Swainson presents the facts in terms of an objective psychology, and her analysis is developed by the direct experience of the medium, Louisa Bennett. The two use the influence of higher forces to explain such things as: how to use the techniques that develop psychic sensitivity, the three phases of psychic development, the three factors that affect communication with your spirit guide, how past life regression can help your current relationships, and how psychic sensitivity and channeling can be used for universal benefit.

ISBN:0-87542-771-5, 168 pgs., 6 x 9, softcover   **$9.95**

WORDS OF POWER
Sacred Sounds of East and West
by Brian & Esther Crowley

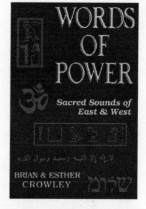

Tune in ... to the hidden "sounds of the soul." Within our human heritage is a vast storehouse of magical words, mantras, invocations and chants handed down from ages past. The ancients used these sacred sounds to still the mind, heal the body, and attain higher states of consciousness. These sounds are their gift to us, and they are revealed at last in this fascinating and instantly usable manual.

Words of Power is the first such work of a universal nature, with a selection of potent sounds in Egyptian, Hebrew, Sanskrit, Tibetan, Arabic, Greek, Latin, English and others. Presented in an easy-to-learn format, *Words of Power* contains simple keys to correct pronunciation, suggested meditations, and detailed explanations of esoteric meanings and functions. This book also explores the origin of the first mantra, the many names of Allah, the important sacred phrase common to all ancient cultures, the meanings of the words of power used by Jesus, and how Moses may have used words of power to part the Red Sea.

ISBN: 0-87542-135-0, 336 pgs., 5 1/4 x 8, illus., softcover   **$12.95**

☽ LOOK FOR THE CRESCENT MOON

Llewellyn publishes hundreds of books on your favorite subjects! To get these exciting books, including the ones on the following pages, check your local bookstore or order them directly from Llewellyn.

ORDER BY PHONE
- Call toll-free within the U.S. and Canada, 1-800-THE MOON
- In Minnesota, call (612) 291-1970
- We accept VISA, MasterCard, and American Express

ORDER BY MAIL
- Send the full price of your order (MN residents add 7% sales tax) in U.S. funds, plus postage & handling to:

  Llewellyn Worldwide
  P.O. Box 64383, Dept. K635-1
  St. Paul, MN 55164–0383, U.S.A.

POSTAGE & HANDLING
(For the U.S., Canada, and Mexico)
- $4 for orders $15 and under
- $5 for orders over $15
- No charge for orders over $100

We ship UPS in the continental United States. We ship standard mail to P.O. boxes. Orders shipped to Alaska, Hawaii, The Virgin Islands, and Puerto Rico are sent first-class mail. Orders shipped to Canada and Mexico are sent surface mail.

International orders: Airmail—add freight equal to price of each book to the total price of order, plus $5.00 for each non-book item (audio tapes, etc.).

Surface mail—Add $1.00 per item.

Allow 4–6 weeks for delivery on all orders.
Postage and handling rates subject to change.

DISCOUNTS
We offer a 20% discount to group leaders or agents. You must order a minimum of 5 copies of the same book to get our special quantity price.

FREE CATALOG

Get a free copy of our color catalog, *New Worlds of Mind and Spirit.* Subscribe for just $10.00 in the United States and Canada ($30.00 overseas, airmail). Many bookstores carry *New Worlds*— ask for it!

Visit our website at www.llewellyn.com for more information.

PSYCHIC EMPOWERMENT FOR HEALTH AND FITNESS
Joe H. Slate, Ph.D.

Can you really "program" your mind during sleep for positive health results the next day? Yes! In the last decade we have learned more about our mental, physical, and spiritual nature than in the past century. In this quest for knowledge we have discovered that our minds hold the power to directly affect our physical health. In fact, the ability of the mind to access the highest dimensions of reality can actually facilitate weight loss, self-control, and, ultimately, optimal fitness. *Psychic Empowerment for Health and Fitness* walks you through a program of psychic exercises that actually can transform your physical body. Your upward spiral to feeling great will begin quickly with Dr. Slate's structured 7-Day Plan for Health & Fitness. You'll tap your mind's deep power and soon experience a relief from stress and anxiety. Find out why psychic protection procedures really are necessary to your health. See for yourself how psychokinesis (PK) and crystals can energize and heal our earth and all her populations. Effect an environmental clearing or a tree power interfusion. The actions you take based on this book will not only benefit you, but our planet as well.

1-56718-634-3, 256 pp., 6 x 9, softcover **$12.95**

FREEDOM FROM THE TIES THAT BIND
The Secret of Self Liberation
Guy Finley

Imagine how your life would flow *without* the weight of those weary inner voices constantly convincing you that "you can't," or complaining that someone else should be blamed for the way *you* feel. The weight of the world on your shoulders would be replaced by a bright, new sense of freedom. Fresh, new energies would flow. *You could choose to live the way* YOU *want.* In *Freedom from the Ties that Bind*, Guy Finley reveals hundreds of Celestial, but down-to-earth, secrets of Self-Liberation that show you exactly how to be fully independent, and *free of any condition not to your liking.* Even the most difficult people won't be able to turn your head or test your temper. Enjoy solid, meaningful relationships founded *in conscious choice*—not *through self-defeating compromise.* Learn the secrets of unlocking the door to your own Free Mind. Be empowered to break free of any self-punishing pattern, and make the discovery that who you really are is already everything you've ever wanted to be.

0-87542-217-9, 240 pp., 6 x 9, softcover   **$10.00**

THE SECRET WAY OF WONDER
Insights from the Silence
Guy Finley
Introduction by Desi Arnaz, Jr.

Discover an inner world of wisdom and make miracles happen! Here is a simple yet deeply effective system of illuminating and eliminating the problems of inner mental and emotional life.

The Secret Way of Wonder is an interactive spiritual workbook, offering guided practice for self-study. It is about Awakening the Power of Wonder in yourself. A series of 60 "Wonders" (meditations on a variety of subjects: "The Wonder of Change," "The Wonder of Attachments," etc.) will stir you in an indescribable manner. This is a bold and bright new kind of book that gently leads us on a journey of Spiritual Alchemy where the journey itself is the destination ... and the destination is our need to be spiritually whole men and women.

Most of all, you will find out through self investigation that we live in a friendly, intelligent and living universe that we can reach into and that can reach us.

0-87542-221-7, 192 pp., 5¼ x 8, softcover   **$9.95**

A RICH MAN'S SECRET
A Novel by Ken Roberts

Victor Truman is a modern-day Everyman who spends his days scanning the want ads, hoping somehow to find his "right place." He has spent years reading self-help books, sitting through "get rich quick" seminars, living on unemployment checks, practicing meditation regimens, swallowing megavitamins, listening to talk radio psychologists … each new attempt at self-fulfillment leaving him more impoverished in spirit and wallet than he was before.

But one day, while he's retrieving an errant golf ball, Victor stumbles upon a forgotten woodland cemetery and a gravestone with the cryptic message, "Take the first step—no more, no less—and the next will be revealed." When Victor turns sleuth and discovers that this stone marks the grave of wealthy industrialist Clement Watt, whose aim was to help spiritual "orphans" find their "right place," he is compelled to follow a trail of clues that Mr. Watt seems to have left for him.

This saga crackles with the excitement of a detective story, inspires with its down-home wisdom and challenges the status quo through a penetrating look at the human comedy that Victor Truman—like all of us—is trying to understand.

1-56718-580-0, 5¼ x 8, 208 pp., softcover   **$9.95**

To order, call 1-800-THE MOON
Prices subject to change without notice

SEVEN SECRETS TO SUCCESS
A Story of Hope
Richard Webster

Originally written as a letter from the author to his suicidal friend, this inspiring little book has been photocopied, passed along from person to person, and even appeared on the internet without the author's permission. Now available in book form, this underground classic offers hope to the weary and motivation for us all to let go of the past and follow our dreams.

It is the story of Kevin, who at the age of twenty-eight is on the verge of suicide after the failure of his business and his marriage. Then he meets Todd Melvin, an elderly gentleman with a mysterious past. As their friendship unfolds, Todd teaches Kevin seven secrets—secrets that can give you the power to turn your life around, begin anew, and reap success beyond your wildest dreams.

1-56718-797-8, 5³⁄₁₆ x 8, 144 pp., softcover   **$6.95**